A Path Through Ohio
A Bicycle Journal

All information presented in this book is for general knowledge and does not constitute direct advice for your own health and safety while enjoying bicycle travel. Please consult your doctor before engaging in cycle travel. This book presents directional advice from maps obtained by the referenced organizations at the time of this trip, since this writing there have been and will continue to be improvements to each trail system. I strongly recommend using the web sites located in the reference section of this book to obtain the current revision of each document before venturing on your own. The ideas in this book are based on my own research and many years of cycling experience along the trail and open road. This work constitutes a good faith effort to capture the sound bites of history and experience gained over these years. I hope you find this story informative and inspires you to take up your bike and explore Ohio.

ISBN 978-0998220406

Introduction

A Path Through Ohio marks a significant decision to break from routine–the routine of office life, the routine of daily training, the routine of the same old breakfast every day for years. In a sense, it is a brief departure from the normality of daily living in an effort to explore the fringes of life buried deep in the dogma of day-to-day existence. It's a return to the freedom offered by solo distance cycling. In 2014 I started traveling south from Cleveland to Columbus, down to Cincinnati and then turning north to Dayton and points beyond, this memoir shares the experiences of a simpler lifestyle on two wheels.

In 1983, as a young and terribly inexperienced solo bike rider clad in sneakers and cut-off sweats and hauling a bunch of camping gear, I took off across the country on a 10-speed bicycle. The trip resulted in an adventure chock-full of memories and fulfilled goals. After a three-decade hiatus, the reasons not to venture out on the open road had become fewer and further between, resulting in an internal desire to re-experience the freedom and spontaneity that only solo bicycle travel seems to satisfy. Exploring untraveled roads rekindled a vaguely familiar mix of feelings including the determination to set and complete a goal–or the fascination of exploring secondary back roads–or the adventure of meeting new people and sharing in their ideas. Now in my

50s, I have arguably slowed down physically (and maybe even mentally, so my friends say). An old, familiar twitch had grown from inside and it was now upon me and challenging me to see if I still had what it takes to return to adventure cycling.

The idea for a trip across Ohio started with a small article written by Susan Glaser and published in the *Cleveland Plain Dealer* in April of 2014. The article celebrated the opening of the Ohio to Erie Trail, (OTET) which had been in development for many years. A series of independent trails throughout the state now connected into a bike path artery now named US Bicycle Route 1. The announcement of the completion of a four-segment bike ride across the state of Ohio was just the motivation I needed to return to the roads by bike.

Through the significant efforts of the *Ohio to Erie Bike Trail Fund* and the Ohio Department of Transportation, a 330-mile path across the state had been created. For years, I had used the independent paths to run or explore in the Dayton area. I had no idea they would eventually form an interconnected trail system free of most automobile traffic. The 88 counties comprising the state of Ohio include a range of geographic diversity from the shores of Lake Erie through the rolling hills of Holmes County- from the significant grades of southeastern Ohio to the state's southern border formed by the Ohio River. Though only a portion of the 88 counties is traveled, the Ohio to Erie Trail cuts across the state's heartland, opening itself up to allow the curious mind to experience a sampling of its terrain, its culture, and its history–a wonderful experience to travel on two wheels. In Xenia, the trail also connects to the western branch of the Erie Canal along the Miami River. The combined paths offer more than 400 miles of green space to travel.

Ohio has a rich history with indigenous Indian tribes dating back well before the European and American interests moved west across the country. *A Path Through Ohio* introduces the reader not only to the state's topography but also to its cultural history. During my travels, I traversed the same land used by many Native American tribes including the Chippewa, the Delaware, the Miami, and the Shawnee. My interest in Ohio's state history was sparked many years ago when reading Allen W. Eckert's *The Frontiersmen*. This tale of a lesser-known (except perhaps to Ohioans and historians) pioneer named Simon Kenton and his acquaintance, the more popular Daniel Boone, became my source of inspiration and reading for many years. Together with the chronicle of the short-lived Erie Canal system, Ohio's rich history and its colorful inhabitants became a source of curiosity for me. This memoir of my travels provides a first-hand narration of the experiences of two-wheel travel through the state. It also allows the reader an opportunity to visualize and experience the landscape that was integral to Ohio's economic development. Along the way, you'll meet the characters and learn of the colorful events in Ohio's history that create a dramatic backdrop to the dynamic scenery of Ohio.

A Path Through Ohio is a trip through Ohio's diverse history and topography from the saddle view of a bicycle. It is an escape from today's 9-to-5 (and often grinding), lifestyle to enjoy the random acquaintance of people that form Ohio's culture. Equipped with three decades of physical training and camping experience, I have honed my open-road survival skills in life and now I am summarizing them for you, the aspiring adventurer. Within this memoir, you will find a layering of what I discovered to be common truths and experiences gathered from solo cycle travel. Along with my stories from the road, these truths are in a literary package called *Looney's Road Rules*. This is a lighthearted way to share with others the skills I obtained and the lessons I learned through years of adventure travel. Each has a deeper meaning for me and, in many cases, was something learned the hard way. It is my desire that it will conjure up your own personal experiences, which could be added to this list. I hope you enjoy this and I look forward to seeing you on the bike paths of Ohio.

Regards,
Mark Looney

A Path Through Ohio
A Bicycle Journal

Mark J. Looney

Day One

Tuesday, July 15
Rocky River to Dalton - 81 miles

The City of Rocky River, Ohio sits on the southern edge of Lake Erie, some eight miles west of Cleveland. Moving to this quaint commuter town four years ago gave my wife and me an easy and wonderful access to the Cleveland Metroparks and their expansive trail system, commonly known as the Emerald Necklace. Within our reach, we also had the cultural arts community in Cleveland and Hopkins International Airport, which I use often for my frequent business travel.

As a career marathoner and triathlete for the past 35 years, the cumulative impact that running on the roads had on my body had begun to take a toll and I realized that my running career was coming to an end. After numerous x-rays and a half dozen doctor visits over as many years, it became clear to me that I was suffering from the ravages of a degenerative, arthritic hip. This condition was already slowing me as a competitor. I was reminded of this physical deterioration each time I laced up for a run. I knew I would have to make some lifestyle changes soon if I were to stay physically fit.

One such change was a return to a 30-year-old practice of distance cycling, which had been a complimentary form of exercise I used to augment my running for some 30 years. The excitement of the wind hissing through my helmet; the exhilaration of blood coursing through my legs; the regaining of my high school metabolism; and the increased range of distances required to satisfy my curiosity of what lies over the next hill or turn all conspired to reawaken my senses to an old friend, the bicycle.

Since 2012 and our move to the Cleveland area, I was gradually replacing running with multi-day road cycling, known today as adventure cycling. Pick a destination on a map, add some elements of the unknown like camping, unpredictable weather, or a chance encounter with a stranger, and you end up with a good old-fashioned adventure just waiting to unfold. The Rocky River Reservation entrance of the Cleveland Metroparks became my new training ground and set the stage for a path through Ohio.

As I stood at the front door of my home, I noticed an uncommon coolness in the lakeside air. A seagull screeched by as a light summer breeze gently blew southeast from the Lake Erie shore. A perfect, sunny, 70-degree day with wispy clouds brushed over a tapestry of blue sky was on tap. The previous week's oppressive temperatures in the 80s and high humidity had set the stage, in my mind, for an uncomfortable journey as I packed a lightweight summer sleeping bag and prepared for a sticky, hot ride across Ohio. Surprisingly, an unexpected polar vortex, usually experienced in the winter but not completely uncommon in the summer months, had dropped down from Canada causing the average temperatures to drop by nearly twenty degrees. This weather phenomenon would eliminate many worries of overheating.

I had never heard of a polar vortex until it was sensationalized by the local news media the night before. Unfortunately, this new weather information did not lead me to an equipment change in sleeping bags from the lightweight fleece to a warmer down bag. This lack of forethought would come to haunt me later in the trip.
It took about an hour to travel from Rocky River to the head of the bicycle trail in Cleveland. My wife Laurie and daughter Erin saw me off on this morning with a familiar look on their face that seemed to say "You're doing this for what reason?" "Don't forget to call me", was the last thing I heard as I rolled down the driveway.

As I rode east down Detroit Road, I found Lakewood in its full pitch fervor for a weekday. As vibrant portions of the city gave way to older, rundown shops and back again, the feel was consistently Cleveland. The intertwined trendy boutiques and restaurants gave the feeling of a gritty city making a resurgence to its glory days. As the early 7:30 start placed me smack in the middle of the city's morning traffic, I found this an uncomfortable beginning for an old-school free spirit. The bold, painted bike lines on the uneven cement and asphalt surface provided a clear path for a safe passage through the city and the traffic showed little objection to my presence. After a half dozen miles down Detroit Road and a right turn onto West 25th street, I quickly spied the tower of the West Side Market that marks the site of the 100-year-old Farmer's Market. Passing the Market immediately tickled my senses as the aroma of fresh bread, the colorful fruit & vegetables, and the floral arrangements made it easy to see how, for decades, pedestrians had been enticed to stop by and enjoy the homegrown fare.

Just past the West Side Market and following a quick left turn onto Lorain Avenue, the Lorain-Carnegie Bridge can be seen crossing the Cuyahoga River and connecting Cleveland's west and east ends as it has since 1932. This iconic bridge was listed on the National Register of Historic Places in 1976 and is a fine example of an Art Deco truss bridge. The pylons, known as the Guardians of Traffic, that flank each end, symbolize the progress in transportation over the past decades. In the 1980s, the bridge was renamed the Hope Memorial Bridge to commemorate its stonemason, William Henry Hope, the man who carved these structures. He also happens to be the father of the popular 20th-century comedian, Bob Hope.

From the south side of the Market, access to Abbey Road is a stone's throw away. The Loraine Abbey intersection leads the biker to a short stint of side-street riding through the trendy Tremont neighborhood. I was tempted to grab a coffee but determined it was too early in the trip to start making this a food binge event.

While passing through Tremont, I could catch glimpses of the Cuyahoga River Valley below. For decades, this was–and remains–the heart of the city's industry, allowing large freighters to pass the winding river on their way to making deposits of ore before returning to the lake. Today, evidence of the deconstruction of the old I-90 Bridge was all around. Iron girders were strewn on either side of the river like an erector set project gone bad. The large span to the other side of the valley was an impressive engineering feat to behold. Down the hill from Tremont lies the Northern Trail entrance by the Alcoa plant at the intersection of Harvard and Jennings Streets. This marks the official start of the Ohio to Erie Trail. (This also represents the end of the trail for those who start southwest in Cincinnati.)

At this point, a little of my biking history might be in order. In July of 1980, a chance encounter with a solo cross-country cyclist became the start of my quest to do the same in 1983. To ride a bicycle was not a particularly cool thing back in those days. Most of my friends from Webster, New York, where I spent my formative years, were muscle car fans. A favorite was the Ford Mustang. To this day, these gear heads have an encyclopedic memory of each car's output and component origination. For me, an interest in exploring the physical limits of human endurance through distance running outweighed the desire for horsepower by mechanical strength (although I must admit that a '66 ragtop Mustang does sit in my garage today). As a young man, the ride across the United States became a dream pinned by a successive series of improvements in physical and mental preparation.

After reading Peter Jenkins' bestseller, *A Walk Across America*, I became intrigued with the solitary lifestyle of a solo traveler. In Jenkins' case, it was a backpacker traveling over 5,000 miles on foot. Employing the patience of a marathoner and the self-reliance of a solo traveler, I took off on my own solo coast-to-coast mission to explore the country. Over the long, quiet miles, I started to form my thoughts of personal conduct while on the road. The underlying theme of endurance sport is learning to endure. In order to endure, one must learn to enjoy from within the activity in which they have engaged. Over time, these evolved into a code of conduct I now refer to as "Looney's Road Rules".

Road Rule Number One: Start every day with a song.

"Begin the day with a friendly voice, a companion unobtrusive, plays that song that's so elusive, And the magic music makes your morning mood"
(Rush, Permanent Waves).

I am a big fan of starting each day with the right attitude in order to gain peak performance from my body. Whether it is the ride into the office or shaking off last night's thundershower while holed up in a tent, the new day brings opportunities to meet new people or to explore one of earth's treasures. As any good athlete prepares for an event, the warm-up is the tool of choice to stretch the body and warm the muscles in preparation for the event. Similarly, the mind needs to warm up. Positive platitudes, visualization exercises, and music are the brain's favorite tools for programming. Although we're not all athletes, starting the day with a positive outlook allows the rider to hop on that saddle just one more time, shake off that cold morning chill, and start churning those pedals to the cadence of a familiar drum beat.

I once had the opportunity to watch the Team USA sprinters warm up for the day's practice at the US Olympic Training Center in Chula Vista, California. From a distance, I watched them jog through their drills on the 400-meter track. At the near end of the beautifully surfaced track was a five-story tower that supported a viewing box and a significant speaker system. As the sprinters concluded their warm-up drills, one came to the tower and blared two audio tracks. The first was a tape from an Olympic stadium with crowd noise as background and the other was the runner's favorite rap music. Inspired by this music, the team went to work immediately.

Each morning before the sun casts its rays upon the road or the grind of another long day is to begin, there is a need to jump-start the solitary spirit of a solo traveler. The best songs are ones that pop into your head without effort. It may be a lyric or a verse that has grabbed the wandering attention of an unsuspecting moment in the past. Often times, it's associated with a strong memory or emotion. In either case, this becomes the cadence and rhythm that encourages the mind and body to work together as one. This road rule was created out of necessity to soften the long, long hours in the saddle. And it is the one, which fills the void created by the lack of human conversation while traveling companionless.

While on Detroit Avenue and passing near the Rock and Roll Hall of Fame, the journey's first song was by an old favorite band of mine. Foreigner, with its lead singer, Lou Graham, was a hometown favorite of Rochester, New York. A vague memory of the lyrics began to cogitate in my mind; "There's a mountain I must climb, feels like a weight upon my shoulder". Gradually, the full song, *I Want to Know What Love Is*, came together in my mind. These opening lyrics described the mood and tone I was feeling while embarking on this latest adventure.

The exhilaration of being on the open road again also brought back some anxiety from my cross-country trip of '83. As a young man thousands of miles from home, the raw emotion of "what the hell are you getting yourself into" was replaced by a calm sense of confidence and determination. I have trained well and hell, I've done this kind of thing before. The bike, weighing in at an easy 35 pounds, is further burdened by an additional 40-pound load of gear and food on the back of the bike. In spite of this load, the bike was manageable. As a matter of science, a fully loaded bike is known to reduce output by up to 20 percent as compared to an unencumbered road bike. My plan was to not expect more than 75 miles per day.

As the feelings of excitement and the prospect of this new adventure began to morph into a business-like cadence on the pedals, so too did the feeling of being exposed to the outdoors and a sense of unbridled exploration. The mid-morning sun on my face, the smell of fresh-cut grass, and the sound of pea gravel grinding underneath my tires all heightened the senses. The odometer reads in the mid-20s and the speedometer is idling at a comfortable speed of 13 to 15 miles per hour. The bike trail has just changed from paved asphalt to crushed limestone. This was the anticipated signal that the Erie Canal towpath had begun. Passing through the city of Independence over a pair of beautifully designed suspension bridges and now passing underneath the Rockside Bridge, the trail plunges the rider into Ohio's history of canal life beginning in the 1820s.

In parallel with the canal is the old Cuyahoga Rail System, which ultimately displaced the long boats and the canal system after a short 30-year competition for dominance. Conveniently located for the rider is the Rockside Train Depot, representing the northern endpoint of a scenic path through the Cuyahoga National Park for both rider and pedestrian. From this point southward toward Akron, the Towpath (and now bike trail) run side-by-side, sharing a common heritage of moving travelers. What was most surprising about today's ride was the ease in pedaling and smoothness of the road surface offered by the crushed limestone. When riding on a traditional path, a rider's undercarriage (my term for a saddle-and-rider interface, also known as the butt, tush, posterior, or derriere) may suffer some discomfort resulting from traveling over occasional bumps and exposed roots on the path. This discomfort can be alleviated somewhat with fat, 38mm road tires. On this particular section of trail, however, after a mere 20 minutes of traversing the comparatively smooth limestone paths, I believe that even the inexperienced rider will find this an enjoyable surface to travel.

As I passed through the city of Independence, there were numerous trailside markers providing details of historically significant communities and a settler's lifestyle along this important waterway. Located just five miles south of Cleveland, this long-inhabited area served as the crossroads for nomadic Indians who roamed the area along the well-established trails of the Muskingum and the Mahoning. Early settlers originally named Independence as a region in which these indigenous Indians of the area and pioneers pushing westward would agree to contentedly coexist in the Cuyahoga River Valley allow for each to hunt, farm, and gain vital resources for survival. With the development of the Erie Canal through this area in the 1850s, the early settlers were replaced by a more industrious brand of settler who used the waterway as a means to move produce and highly valued sandstone used for gristmills. This commerce ultimately placed Independence on the map of modern importance. The trail offers many opportunities to carefully examine the remains of locks used to control the water flow and depth, which allowed the long boats to travel in either direction. In some cases, the lock keepers' residence may be found nearby. As with much of Ohio's transportation history, trails gave way to canals, which were shortly followed thereafter by rail. Nearly 400 years later, Independence continues to serve as a major crossroad for commerce as the intersections of I-77 and I-480 take travelers through this historic region. Meanwhile, on bike, the passage of history unfolds while riding along some of the original paths created by our ancestors.

As the trail turns south, a distinct change in the scenery is seen with mature tree coverage replacing the open grasslands. This makes for a pleasant canopy and protection from the sun. While passing through the trails, I soon found myself in the middle of a group ride for children sponsored by Century Cycle, a local bicycle shop. Watching the little daredevils weave in and around my "big rig" brought a grin to my face as I was reminded of a more youthful time. This young bike enthusiast left no mud puddle untouched, nor was a child left without a mud stripe up his backside. The inquisitive kids quickly moved to one side or the other of the trail as I gently announced my riding up through the rear of their pack. Having survived my encounter with the younger set and without significant fanfare or any national park signage, I discovered that I was entering the Cuyahoga Valley National Park.

Arriving at the small trailside town of Boston Mills, I came upon a quaint farm home now turned Visitor Center for the National Park Service. An inviting wrap-around porch with white rocking chairs facing the trail created in me a certain temptation for a seat of a different kind. While peering through the floor-to-ceiling pane glass windows, an intriguing landscape model of a nearby lock and long boat construction business was found. Upon further investigation inside the Visitor Center, I happened upon a reduced-size, cut-away model of a long boat. The cut-away exposed the meticulous mortise-and-tenon joinery necessary to create these 90-foot long passenger and freight vessels.

Shortly after leaving Boston Mills, I encountered a farm stand. In reality, it was more like an open-door farmer's market with a wide range of fruits and vegetables. Everything was fresh and colorful. With little thought, this became my first official lunch stop of the trip. In front of the market was a parking area for a spin-off business of "try and like" wooden lawn gliders for sale. As I was gliding back and forth, eating fresh peaches in the sun, it became apparent that the Amish carpenters, with their famed woodworking skills, were onto a brilliant marketing technique using the proximity of the towpath as a means of commerce for their products. The gliders were comfortable and an easy distraction for the weary biker. "Is that cash or charge? Delivery or pick up?"

After lunch, the miles started to roll by pretty easily along the crushed gravel path. The midday sun tried to pierce through the heavy forest canopy with selected leaves exploding in color as the backlight of the sun struggled to reach the ground. Hats off to the National Park Service for their meticulous care of the trail and surrounding beauty. After passing through the city and now being immersed in the natural beauty of the National Park and the perfect weather conditions, the full enjoyment of riding through this outdoor treasure was becoming a reality of the Ohio to Erie Trail.

Gradually, the signs for exiting the national park gave way to the city of Akron. Now in the outskirts of northern Akron, frequent street crossings provided clues that the uninterrupted crushed gravel pathway was soon to end. While passing through the city of Akron, I was impressed with the care taken to mark the path with a red dashed line for those of us just passing through town. This minimized the confusion of intersecting bike paths and co-use streets as bike lanes. The path carefully passes through the city and wraps around the outfield of the minor league baseball stadium, which is home to the Akron Rubber Ducks, an AA feeder team to the Cleveland Indians. Clearly, this was a well laid-out city path designed to showcase the city's offerings and beauty. The southern part of Akron continued to display its impressive trailway through the use of carefully constructed boardwalks along Summit Lake and the interconnecting waterways forming the Portage Trail System by way of canoe. The informational placards posted along the trail provide a deep history of the region's importance. This was a common start and end-point for an eight-mile long portage used by the Cuyahoga and Tuscarora Indians for seasonal hunting. Though a north-south passage to the Ohio River was desired, the topography of the region and increased elevation caused these ancient travelers to carry their gear from one point to another for eight miles in order to reach their destination. Likewise, the engineers of the early 1820s recognized the same problem although their solution was a bit different. They chose to dig the canal deeper and developed locks to artificially raise the water level, allowing boats to pass through the higher elevation.

Not far from the bike path, at a busy intersection, is a life-size monument of an Indian carrying his canoe, providing a snapshot of the arduous journey performed seasonally in order to access fertile hunting grounds. After reading the historical marker, I could not help but feel being drawn back in time as the bike path retraced the ancient trail used by these early inhabitants. The only difference was that I was going to roll along the trail with my gear lashed to my bike, rather than carrying it on my back. Modernization has its benefits.

As the miles rolled by, numerous locks most in disrepair, became a good reason to take pause and note the manual labor that was required to dig the miles of waterway. The city of Canal Fulton retains much of its historic feel as the towpath parallels the main street through town. One of the only active long boat companies in existence continues to provide visitors with an opportunity to experience the pace and lifestyle of canal life. Draft horses are fed and maintained along the towpath and are interchanged as each tour down the river and back is completed. When time is available, this quaint town atmosphere is worth a second visit to explore further.

While passing through the Canal Fulton Park, I had an opportunity to observe some of the logistical challenges encountered after some 150 years of technological advances. With a dozen or more guests fully loaded on a reconditioned long boat, three young men–the operators–struggled mightily to turn the boat around in a tight portion of the canal in order to load the next set of guests. Against my nature to pitch in and help, I chose to stay in the background and not get recruited. Meanwhile, as the struggle to straighten the boat continued, the pole-men used a combination of ropes, pole pushing, and body weight to gradually find a wider notch in the canal in which to swing the boat 180 degrees, allowing the guests to disembark. The entire operation of turning the vessel lasted well over 45 minutes, much too long for this casual observer. The park also contained a dry-docked long boat, allowing visitors to inspect the workmanship of these antique vessels. It was well worth the stop to gain a perspective of the early freight and mass transit system at work. At least no one had to portage his vessel through this area.

Leaving Canal Fulton and continuing on, I parked my bike at a working lock with a historic marker. While taking pictures for my research, I started a conversation with an older lady and her grandson. She was very interested in the ride to Cincinnati. We talked about common points of interest along the trail and she told me how she would like to "take up her bike" and ride the trail some day. I encouraged her to plan a ride with her grandson as a bonding opportunity.

Miles later, after entering the Sippo Valley, another rider passed me by. All I saw was a white sunbonnet, rolled up jeans, and an obnoxious bike bell that was used liberally to clear the trail. I nearly jumped out of my skin when the rider lay on the bell as she passed by. I eventually caught up with

26

her and we engaged in a long game of leapfrog; passing and re-passing each other numerous times. I introduced myself after the second pass. We rode together long enough that Betty had the time to explain, before she sped off ahead of me, that she was an active 70-year-old woman on a mission. I liken this to old-fashioned speed dating. As this comical parade continued for many miles, I was curious about her motivation to ride so fast so I pressed my pace again and finally caught back up to her.

I asked, "Where are you headed?" With brevity of words and a sense of determination, she said that she wanted to get to McDonald's before it closed because they had a sale on chocolate-dipped ice cream cones for 50 cents. It was over 30 years ago that I remember devouring two to three ice cream cones at a time from Mickey D's. It always made for a great afternoon treat while pedaling around. As I was trying to catch old Betty–and also trying to catch my breath–she turned off the path in the Sippo Valley Trail. As she reached the bridge rampart into Massillon, she gave me a "beauty queen" wave goodbye and was off to McDonalds.

The day was pushing towards four in the afternoon and I had hit my self-imposed, first day limit of 75 miles. In a way, this was a physical self-discovery as I had not been on a loaded bike for many years and was not looking to push the limits of reasonableness. I began to look for a place to settle down for the evening. As 75 miles crept to 80, I was starting to feel the fatigue of a good day's effort and found myself anxious to find a quiet spot along the trail to open up my tent for the evening. I passed a couple of beautiful, man-made lakes, each one very enticing for a dip. One pond was particularly inviting and had a camp right by the trail. At the opposite end of this large acreage was a dog kennel business with an attached cabin. As I pulled alongside the pond to wash the days salt off my face, I noticed the kennel owner staring at me from her backyard deck. Another biker passing by saw the possible conflict and suggested I knock on the door and ask if a pitched tent at the far end would be allowed for such a beautiful spot.

Trekking back a quarter of a mile, I had an uneasy feeling. The dogs in the kennel, clearly aware of my presence, got excited. I anticipated that the owner was ready for me. She answered my knock on the front door whereupon I politely complimented her on the property and described the nature of my travels. I asked if it would be acceptable for me to set up a tent at the far end of the pond. Unfortunately, I received a firm response of "I don't feel comfortable with that". Then she started quizzing me; where did I start from; how valid was my cross-state story? Withering under her insistent cross-examination, I decided to give up on this spot. Sometimes the juice is just not worth the squeeze. A couple of miles down the path, I discovered a more hospitable site for camping. I pitched my tent in a clearing in the woods just a few feet from the path and started to wind down for the evening.

The first night's dinner was unappetizing as I unpacked an old "Meal Ready to Eat", also known quite efficiently as an MRE. This relic was left over from Hurricane Katrina disaster in New Orleans back in 2005, had been given to me by a Boy Scout friend who had volunteered there. The nine-year-old meal was carefully pulled apart and ingested for its calorie value only. The meal went down about as well as my initial effort for the first night's rest. The temperatures were mild as I sat down to summarize day one's fulfilling events. Interestingly, from my spot, I remained undetected as the evening trail walkers passed by me.

Road Rule Number Two. Make a journal entry daily.

"There are a thousand thoughts lying within a man that he does not know till he takes a pen to write."
William Thackeray.

Summarize each day by making a conscious effort to capture the day's highlights or possibly the low points, the associated feelings, and the key learning. "Hell, I'll never do that again" may be just the note needed to prevent you from repeating the same mistake over. Each is a gem of an emotion to be recalled at a later point in time.

Journal writing in the privacy of your own space allows for free-flowing thoughts to be captured and, if desired, articulated more creatively at a later point. Surprisingly, some of my best moments of self-discovery and observation occur after a long day in the saddle with dinner in the tank and the evening sun fading on the horizon. Take the time to jot, draw, or scribble your likes and dislikes, how you felt, or maybe even a new bucket list idea. As Victor Frankl, a Holocaust survivor once wrote, "Writing allows us to free ourselves from our history". In part, I think he was trying to convey that the simple act of documenting our feelings allows us to move on in life to enjoy or suffer new feelings, making for a richer life experience.

Journaling after a long and eventful day was a practice my father insisted on many years ago. The thoughtful characterization of images and experiences has served as a gentle reminder of a day of memorable moments from the road. A sunny day that it seemed would never end is one such memory I shall not forget. Remembering Road Rule Number Two, I put down my pen around 8:30 and rested on top of my sleeping bag. The mild air was a bit sticky from the day's heat but the colors of the bent wheat changed as a gentle breeze passed through the field.

Day Two

Wednesday, July 16
Dalton to Mt. Liberty - 76 miles

Early in the morning, a rustling in the brush and a snorting sound in the cool darkness piqued my awareness from within the frail protection of my tent. Half annoyed and half troubled, I stayed wrapped within the warmth of my sleeping bag as I made my observations. From outside my tent came another series of hoarse snorts from what sounded like a disgruntled creature. Carefully listening to each strange noise, I gathered that whatever my morning visitor was, it was pacing back and forth in an effort to express its discontent. Now sitting upright, I planned my exit strategy in the event the creature took a more aggressive stance with me, its transgressor. While weighing my options, this experience reminded me of Road Rule Number Three.

Road Rule Number Three: Sleep with one eye open.

"You must stop and turn to face the dragon, to realize he is made of paper" (Chinese Proverb)

In today's world of verbal diarrhea on TV and bad news which sells best, our society is swept into a condition of fear; fear of walking the dog around the block; fear to go to the "east side" or "that" place. Fortunately, the cyclist does not run into this amped shock culture very often. For some, their fears are more founded in urban America rather than the woods of rural America. Yes, there are bears and deer and other wild critters out there that forage for food at night. In our mind's eye, we have a tendency to explode the snapping of a twig or a hearty snort of a buck as a threat and imminent danger that may be lurking in the dark. "Sleeping with one eye open" simply means to be aware of your surroundings and take appropriate precautions. Remove your food from your tent, don't camp near animal feces or tracks, and stay away from freshly dug holes or hollowed timber. Finally, when you first begin camping, you will likely only get partial sleep through most of your camp nights. These fears generally pass as your confidence grows with your capabilities and surroundings.

The camping part of adventure cycling is not for everyone. Consequently, there are many reasonable options to pursue. Plan ahead. Make sure your accommodations are confirmed the day before you arrive. Get cleaned up and sleep well. You will have the same challenges the next day as those who chose the ground upon which to sleep.

I have the greatest regard for those who have responded to the call of adventure. Those of you who have experienced this form of travel will likely attest that there is a vast network of bike shops that exhibit a general openness to help a fellow traveler. You're never really alone. The sandbox in which you play is just a little larger than most others.

Having spent many a night in unsecured locations, it has proven beneficial to maintain a level of consciousness that is at the ready. For a lone cyclist, this is generally a "flight" rather than "fight" decision. With this disruptive and what I feared to be aggressive noise, I had to take stock of the situation and determine my next move. After careful thought, I deduced that I had pissed off some large animal, likely a deer or a cow. I decided that I would be best served to stay put and wait out the disruption through the balance of the morning while trying to get a little more shut-eye. Staring at the roof of my little pup tent and waiting for the sun to hit the treetops around me was not my idea of a good use of time. The pensive night's sleep left me with thoughts of the upcoming day's ride and caused me to rethink my decision to delay my departure. I decided to make an early and quick up-and-out after all. While rolling up my wet tent, I found a matted-down area of grass and some deer prints in the nearby mud. I guessed that this was likely the calling card of my early morning intruder.

Back on the bike path and pedaling by 6:40 am, I found the route into Dalton poorly marked due to recent construction. As the familiar cadence of pedal spinning returned to its groove, the early sun's rays appeared from behind my back. A surreal orange glow seeped through the trees, casting long shadows, which distorted the size of the trees and my own bike. To my right were the iconic, rolling cornfields of Ohio with the hint of early morning dew over the field. The corn stalks were about four feet in height and glistened as the moisture on the leaves caught the sun's rays. A short time later, I came into Dalton and found a designated restroom in the village's vacated ballpark where I proceeded to indulge in a "bird bath" cleaning. Ah, the small pleasures of adventure camping.

Dalton before eight in the morning was pretty uneventful. I found the sleepy village to be unprepared for this early morning traveler. Having missed the day's breakfast or coffee, I wolfed down a handful of nuts and raisins and washed it down with water while riding through the deserted streets. I would later regret my decision to forgo a real breakfast, as the anticipated hills of Holmes County took more fuel than I had expected.

These challenging hills belong to the Amish. The houses were well maintained and gave the appearance of a simple lifestyle. Laundry drying on the line, beautifully manicured and colorful front yard gardens, single-room schoolhouses, bearded men walking the county roads with apparent determination and, of course, the black, horse-drawn carriages all suggested a land frozen in time.

After an hour in the saddle since Dalton and having endured a couple of significant climbs, the hunger pangs were starting to return. In need of breakfast, I started searching for anything that appeared edible. Finally, I came across a "bump and dent" grocery store. As I entered the store, I noticed two impeccably dressed Amish children at the door. The boy was clad in blue jean overalls and the girl in a prairie dress. Both were shoeless and each was staring at me with a wide-eyed awe, almost as if I were the legendary Bigfoot sometimes reported to being seen in areas like this. I think we were each caught by surprise as the bohemian look of a cyclist generally tends to a more utilitarian look than with which most are comfortable. I was, of course, trying to assess the children's curiosity as they watched me peruse possible purchases in each of the half-dozen aisles of groceries.

As I stepped forward to settle up for my purchase, the children were asked by a parent to step aside. This request was made in German, the primary language spoken in the Amish community. After a 20-minute shopping spree, my only purchase ended up being a six-pack of a popular brand-name breakfast drink that went down easily at first but later was found to have a terrible aftertaste, especially while drinking on the ride. I threw the remainder of the six-pack into my deep storage pannier. This unsatisfying concoction would eventually find its home in a convenient garbage can in the miles to come.

Meanwhile, the hills of Holmes County were gradually taking a toll on this loaded rider (85 pounds of bike and gear). By 11 am, I had covered only 20 miles. I was fortunate to enjoy favorable weather as I passed through this area. The day's temperature never exceeded 70 degrees, making for comfortable climbing up and down these wonderfully challenging hills. Along the way, I cracked a smile upon seeing a mother, in full Amish dress and with two young boys in tow, pushing a child in a baby carriage. Each boy would take his turn gleefully pulling the other in a handmade rickshaw styled as a black, horse-drawn carriage.

After a half day of travel in Holmes County, I grew wise to riding in the tracks of the horse-drawn buggies. These tracks, hardened from repeated contact with the buggy's steel-clad wheels, were much smoother than the rest of the trail and provided for much faster travel. And then there was the added advantage of avoiding the horse poop found between the two carriage tracks. Rolling my way into Fredericksburg, I experienced the positive effects of Road Rule Number Four.

Road Rule Number Four: For every hill, there is an equal and opposite hill.

Having logged thousands of miles on bike and on foot, I have learned not to fight or become obsessed with the topography and the elements that Mother Nature and fate have put in my path. Standing in frustration at the base of a mountain or staring in the face of dark, foreboding clouds does not change the reality that you must either endure or go home. Rather, be prepared for the extremes and take action in advance to maintain reasonable comfort during tough times. For those of faith, these are the character-enriching experiences that you are in search of. It is God's way of shaping you to use your gifts, turning fear and humility into courage and accomplishment. The silver lining of each experience is that there is a downhill ride and a sunny side to each challenge.

In this case, I had paid ahead with the hills for the entire morning and it was now time to reap the rewards of a nice, long glide into town. I came to the main intersection and the only traffic light in Fredericksburg. The early ride without breakfast had left me nearing the equivalent of caloric fumes. The unpleasant breakfast drink and trail mix reserves were an insufficient source of fuel to power up and down the Holmes County hills.

Road Rule Number Five: Know thy food and water needs.

Dietary and hydration concerns are always prevalent when one is exposed to the elements regardless of whether that exposure is just for hours or for trips lasting multiple days. Of the two, hydration is your number one concern in order to maintain proper body fluid levels. I have noticed that the combination of exposure and exercise can best be compensated with up to one liter per hour of water. When urinating, look for a clear fluid as an indication of your success. I also alternate water with sports drinks when on a particularity long grind to help replace lost electrolytes.

The calories burned (CB) during a long day's journey are also an important statistic to watch while actively riding. There are many calculators on the Internet that estimate the amount of CB during exercise. I suggest consulting your doctor before embarking on a journey. There are many variables that dictate your physiological needs on a given day. There is much more science behind the maintenance of your physical needs. As you become familiar with any form of distance exercise, be aware of your unique needs and replace calories and fluids regularly. I prefer ice cream any time the opportunity avails itself.

Plan ahead, know the distances between stops and if they are greater than a couple of hours, plan to pack extra reserves. Through force of habit, I generally carry two water bottles and

energy bars as a reserve. Let your body be your first indicator to
replace fluids and fuel.

———————————◦◦◦———————————

As the creator of these invaluable road rules, you would think I would be more inclined to follow them but in this case, you would be wrong. In this particular case, I was definitely on Code Yellow and nearing Red. In years past, close friends and family members had affectionately adopted a coding system describing my appetite. Code Green implied a general comfort level while Code Yellow was indicative of a half-hour warning and Code Red meant system shutdown. In contemporary cycling terms, this is known as "bonking". I was in need of calories of any type and, fortunately, Fredericksburg delivered.

Entering Fredericksburg was a bit like stepping back in time 75 years. The local gas station had been converted into a drive-through restaurant and was waiting for me to refuel. After a quick purchase of doughnuts, OJ, and an apple, I started to devour my calorie-rich breakfast. Halfway through my grazing, I was interrupted by Lisa, a talkative senior with one of those undeniable personalities who interjected herself into my mealtime. "Well, you missed the crowds we had here two weeks back", she blurted. Without my asking her to elaborate, she continued, saying that the GOBA bike ride had come through town two weeks prior.

Having completed the GOBA in past years with my son, I knew she was referring to the Great Ohio Bike Adventure. This is an event in which some 3,000 bike-riders trek through a 300 to 400-mile course that winds its way through a selected quadrant of the state. The riders swarm into town, each consuming hundreds of calories in a single sitting. It's a great economic boost for any volunteer group or small restaurant that is fortunate enough to be on the GOBA route. Lisa, a former restaurant owner, was not shy about initiating conversation with me. She was also certainly not shy about making known her opinion of the local Amish, either. She liked them and informed me that there are three levels of Amish; high, medium, and low, and each interacts with the public in different ways.

As we continued our conversation, I realized that Lisa's comments revealed a much more insightful respect for the Amish. As an elderly, white-bearded man with a traditional straw hat walked by, Lisa interrupted herself in mid-sentence and blurted, "Hey Frank, how's it going?" The Amish gentleman waved his coffee mug as if to salute and returned the greeting, never intending to disrupt our conversation. I later found that Holmes County contains the highest population of Amish in the country and likely the world, estimated at 36,000. Their common language is a combination of Pennsylvania Dutch and German. Perhaps this explains why the kids back at the bump and dent store were apparently speechless when I entered. And here, I thought it was my bike garb.

With a whole lot more biking ahead and my bio-clock screaming to get a move-on, I was looking for an easy conversation change. Although probably not the best choice of topic changes, I was really curious about her earlier observations and the three levels of Amish. Like many religious groups, there is a majority who are active participants following their creed. There is also a devout branch adhering to the tenants of simple work and placement on earth to serve God's interests. Then there are those who take a more casual view of God's purpose and assume a more practical approach to automation when work is required.

Without much more than a handshake, Lisa and I parted. I like to think that we each left with a memory and perspective that we did not have before our meeting. In this particular instance, I think I received the larger portion of perspective and that is exactly why the travel is worthwhile.

Getting back on the road after an interesting conversation, it usually takes a few minutes for me to find my pedal groove and start spinning again. After a few light turns of the pedals (or chain ring for the experienced cyclist) and heading out of Fredericksburg, the road quickly turned into a co-use road, shared between an uncommon pairing of pedestrians and Amish horse buggies only. Car traffic was absent on this full-width road. Yellow diamond signs with a black silhouette of a horse carriage were positioned along the road as it passed through an expansive wetland. On both sides of the road, a vast plain of jade lily pads with white blossoms floated on the water's surface. Occasionally, my eye was caught by proverbial bumps on a log–box turtles sitting side-by-side while soaking in the afternoon sun. The steady croaking of frogs created a natural symphony that was the perfect accompaniment to the serene setting of the marsh. I greatly enjoyed traversing the flat miles as nature's bounty unfolded. Below the surface of this vast marsh was an ecosystem with hundreds of native plant and animal species actively engaged in an intertwined spiral of co-existence. Though the surface was calm, there was a certain subtle energy given off. It may have been the bubbles from beneath the beaver dam that appeared on the surface of the marsh. Maybe it was the birds of prey perched on a high limb or the careful stepping of the Blue Heron along the banks of the marsh. Whatever it was, there was a sense that something was about to happen, if only one was patient enough to stop, listen, and observe. As the marsh gradually gave way to a more wooded terrain, the canopy of trees again protected the ground from the sun's penetrating rays. It was clear that this portion of raised bike path was created through the sweat equity of the canal diggers of years back and which eventually yielded to the train line.

A sign for the town of Killbuck was an indication that food supplies would soon be within reach. An old wooden train station depot painted in yellow, now faded, and showed signs of disrepair and overgrowth. I snapped a picture of the town sign thinking there were many more to come, with each having a story behind it. Back in a day when travel moved at a slower pace through the Ohio woodlands, the depots were the first sign for the traveler that civilization was approaching. Killbuck, and so many other small towns along the line prospered by the canal and later by the trains.

As the bike path continued further south, small villages like Killbuck, nestled in the rolling hills, reminded me of similar towns and country roads I had traveled through in West Virginia. It also brought to mind a famous song written by John Denver, "Take Me Home, Country Roads". I recognized a comforting sense of transparency with open screen doors, curtains blowing in the midday breeze, and a friendly level of pedestrian traffic on the main street. Riding through town, I spied an older gentleman dressed as a rhinestone cowboy, complete with belt buckle, a turquoise bolo tie, and an old pickup truck nearby. I was surprised to see that he was holding the attention of a group of youngsters outside of a small grocery store. Some were seated on their bikes, some on the tabletop and even more sitting on the bench seat. I was curious and intrigued as to how this unlikely group came about. Meanwhile, my stomach was gurgling again so I decided to park my bike against a railing adjacent to the picnic tables and this gathering of youngsters. The little roadside store did not have much from which to choose and I hastily chose a burger and a Gatorade. I was eager to get back outside to eavesdrop on the conversation. As I listened in, I was not surprised to learn that the nattily dressed gentleman had once been a schoolteacher. The old-timer was engaging each of the kids by name and covering everything from their favorite football teams to computer apps.

At one point, a little girl asked what kind of bike I was riding. I explained that it takes me on long trips and that all my gear is contained in the saddlebags bags in the back. The older gentleman was equally curious about my arrival to Killbuck and asked about my starting point. He was a lifetime resident of the town and appeared to find enjoyment in reaching across multiple generations and learning the simple pleasures of a youngster just released from school for the summer. It seemed as if the retired schoolteacher and the curious children enjoyed the companionship of one another. Before I had finished my lunch, a pair of female riders pulled into town from the west on Route 520. They were on day five of a trip from Cincinnati and explained that in my near future as I headed southeast the hills were about to return. In particular, they informed me that the immediate climb out of Killbuck on Route 62 was a doozy. As they reported their trip, a pit in my stomach was forming. Had I possibly miscalculated my days of travel from Cleveland to Cincinnati? Were the forthcoming hills more than I anticipated? Was I now looking at five to six days? Nonetheless, the challenge called and I pedaled on out of town looking for the Route 62 climb.

As the main street took a few turns out of Killbuck, I found my inside voice humming an old Glen Campbell tune, "Rhinestone Cowboy". It wasn't long before I was staring up at the hill the two riders in town had forecast in my near future. I quickly slid my hands down on the shift levers of the bike, switching into the granny gear, the smallest gear associated with the pedals of my bike, to ensure a successful climb up this monstrous hill. I was determined to pedal my way up and, at numerous times, had to raise my upper body from the saddle to jog on the pedals in an effort to maintain my uphill momentum. After a good effort and a moderate case of oxygen debt, I found myself cheating a glance back down the monster hill as a reward for the effort. I was soon to learn that there were many more hills yet to come.

On one such hill, I saw a large, human-like figure standing alongside the road as it slowly came into view. The silhouette provided few details but it carried a rather odd hunch to its

46

posture. As I continued past this motionless figure and on through the open and rolling hills of the Ohio pasturelands, I realized that I had just crossed paths with the mystical Bigfoot. Right here in Holmes County, Ohio. No kidding! A life-sized, 10-foot, concrete Bigfoot statue was poised outside a fabrication factory on this old country road. Sure enough, around the corner were a dozen or more baby (smaller) Bigfoot statues. I couldn't help but laugh at the poor guy who brings home one of these lawn ornaments–"Hey Honey, look what I found!" At best, maybe a statue of Bigfoot could be used as a good college dorm prank.

Even with the hills out of Killbuck behind me, I could still feel the resultant searing pain in my legs. Remembering Road Rule Number Four, (*For every hill there is an equal and opposite hill*), the southbound route along US 62 provided a nice payback in the form of an easy descent into the Mohican Valley Trail. Along the way, signs for the state's "Longest Covered Bridge", aka The Bridge of Dreams, were seen. Of course, it can be expected that anything in this part of the state worth visiting requires a hill climb first. At the top of the trail, the path continues across the 200-meter bridge, clearly designated for pedestrian traffic only. I was amazed to see a couple on a three-wheeled motorcycle–commonly referred to as a trike–with a trailer in tow, trying numerous times to ride their vehicle across the bridge. Each attempt they made resulted only in them getting pinched off by the narrowness of the bridge walls as they battled with the girth of their vehicle. Another couple and I watched as the riders finally came to the conclusion that this was not a good idea. It was a classic case of one's eyes being too big for the stomach. The trike couple finally gave up and turned their vehicle around to exit the park in the same direction from which they had come.

Once the bridge was cleared, the pedestrian traffic was able to enjoy the converted train track high above the streambed. The following miles on the Mohican Valley Trail were a bit disappointing as much of the trail was dirt and mud, making for a difficult traverse on a loaded bike. I have since read that this section of trail is now completed and much easier to navigate.

As the day drifted along, I discovered that a number of train depots had been converted to convenient rest stations for pedestrian traffic. From a historical perspective, these were the connection points for numerous towns that developed into economic centers for commerce and human transport across Ohio. After a short, 30-year lifespan, the locomotive largely replaced the Erie Canal system. Over time, the complications of flooding and low water levels proved the locomotive to be a more reliable form of transportation. Combined with the carrying capacity and speed benefits of rail, the Ohio legislators began to redirect funding in support of the train before the canals were completely developed. Whether by train or by boat, the names of destinations such as Killbuck, Danville, Mount Vernon, Sunbury, Gambier, Westerville, and Columbus became intersecting points of trade and commerce. In many locations along the trail, the side-by-side legacy of each mode of transportation had given way to the bike path. With your eyes closed and the assistance of a gentle breeze, you just may hear the sound of the conductor or captain calling out these town names that will forever echo in the woods as you pedal from point to point.

As the Mohican Valley Trail merges into the Kokosing Gap Trail further to the west, a particularly beautiful section of mature Ohio woodland awaits the rider west of Kenyan College and Gambier Township. The bike trail takes advantage of the now-retired rail system and has numerous overhead bridge structures standing as out-of-place in the forest as monoliths, representative of a time long since its prime. I pulled into Mount Vernon in the mid afternoon and decided to grab dinner at a restaurant where I hoped to plug in my electronic gadgets. My new cell phone had not been tested and was already out of juice. Of course, this is a slap in the face of Road Rule Number Six.

Road Rule Number Six: Let go of the electronics, use your surroundings, and use your senses.

"Baby, be a simple, really simple man. Oh, be something you love and understand." Lynyrd Skynyrd, Simple Man

This is not about the resistance to using electronics or popular GPS and experience-enhancing tools. It is about raising your awareness to your experiences. As our technology gets better and better, it also insulates us from our immediate surroundings. It hides in plain sight and can make us oblivious to danger. If you're staring at your GPS, you're losing out not only on the immediate scenery but also may be unaware of that pothole in the road just 10 feet in front of you. Put the watch away. Watches are used for keeping appointments. Some of the best days on the road have a start and end point with the rising and setting of the sun. Allow the entire course of the day to be a series of random and unexpected events.

The last time I checked, your body will tell you when to eat, sleep, and relieve yourself. It's okay to find a park during a midday ride, pull up under a broad-leafed oak to take shelter from the mid afternoon sun, and just take a nap. You're on autopilot now. You may just find that the slice of freedom from your highly structured and complex "other life" is what you have been craving for years.

In case you were wondering, I used to be old school; maps and compass all the way. However, with the usefulness of GPS units as well as safety issues that are often addressed by the use of these devices, navigating areas with sometimes interchangeable street names and confusing route numbers can be less complicated than the old school way of having to refer to old, outdated maps and route numbers for guidance and direction. In the name of full disclosure, it is quite likely that I will include a GPS unit in my gear on my next cycling adventure.

———————————

Road Rule Number Six, talks about using your surroundings and your senses. While usually a very good rule to follow, on this ride–and with executive authority–I decided to modify this rule in the event of an emergency. With my wife's parting words, "Don't forget to call", in mind, this was all the reason I needed for the modification.

A hot and dusty wind blowing across the Mount Vernon streets gave the town the feel of the classic Clint Eastwood spaghetti western, *The Good the Bad and the Ugly*, with the familiar flute piece repeating itself. All that was needed to complete the Western drama was for tumbleweed to blow across my path. Circling around the city block a couple times, I decided to eat dinner at a local pizza shop. I was hot, salty, and parched and consequently was escorted to a corner table away from the other guests. Once seated, I proceeded to spread out my maps and plug in my electronic toys. With a cold pitcher of lemonade on the table sweating with condensation and a pizza on the way, the evening was starting to feel complete.

It was 6 pm and the summer solstice was pushing the sunset back to nearly 9 pm on Ohio's western border. I had a few more sunlight hours to kill and nothing but the open road to help burn up that large pizza. With a relaxing pace, I found myself with 20 miles of post-dinner riding and acres of wistful wheat waving in the breeze. Finally, the coming darkness encouraged me to set up camp. Once settled in, I started putting pencil to paper as the sun cast its long shadows over the rolling field.

Unfortunately, the peaceful evening was short-lived as the return of the dreaded snorting blasts from an upset deer became the early morning's intonation... again. A couple of glances through the tent screening revealed nothing but an unusually cool night with a full moon casting a glaze over a fog-covered field. With a second disrupted night's sleep, I was feeling unusually punchy. This led me to the humorous explanation that the same buck from the night before had been following me for the past 80 miles along the bike path and was here to haunt me again. This time, I muffled my ears with some loose clothing and fought for a few more moments of sleep.

Day Three

Thursday, July 17
Mount Liberty to South Charleston - 105 miles

After another disruptive night's sleep, I realized that the unseasonably cool evenings and insufficient bedding had me waking up tired and irritable. Clearly, I have should have made the last minute adjustment and brought my goose-down sleeping bag instead of the fleece. Regardless of the restless night, the road was waiting and a dark 6:30 start saw the first rotation of wheels.

A new headlight for the bike is proving to be the MacGyver tool of the trip as it doubles for evening and morning light assistance–no flashlight necessary. The blackness of the early morning surrounded my passage through the trail and was alleviated with the assistance of my single beam headlight. Slowly, the song of the day eases into my foggy memory; "Up with the sun, gone with the wind. She always said I was lazy". With a quick passing of the morning ride, I pieced together the rest of the words to Bob Seger's "Traveling Man".

Traveling towards Centerburg, I passed through the appealing village of Hartford, Ohio. The small village center consisted of a green, about an acre in size, with an older town hall building centered on the lawn. An original water pump was still working and served me well to refresh my water bottles. A well-worn city block with shops and private residences intertwined surrounded the green. All of this gave the ambiance of an old colonial village similar to those I had seen on my bike travels through rural Connecticut. The tight-knit community surrounding the green had not awoken as I walked around the block. The realization of a fresh breakfast was going to elude me again and I opted for the usual nuts and fruit stored away in one of the pockets of my panniers.

Soon after leaving the colonial New England experience in Ohio, I rode into the town of Sunbury, an old stagecoach town with its beginnings dating back to the early 1800s. For decades, Sudbury was the intersection of two major routes, the Walhonding Trail and the Delaware Newark Pike. This Midwestern town saw the likes of William Henry Harrison, Rutherford Hayes, and Johnny Appleseed. Today, the town boasts the historic Sunbury Inn and a larger town hall and green similar to the green I had admired in Hartford, again taking a New England-styled ambiance.

For my immediate fuel needs, an old-fashioned 50's era doughnut shop served as a perfect stopping point to grab breakfast. While savoring my second cup of java, I took stock of my body ailments and noticed that my knees were a bit achy. However, I was pleasantly surprised to note that my hips had not been aggravated by all the activity. It's a common joke amongst my running friends that my 50,000-mile warranty had been exceeded following a 35-year running career. So far, the bike is allowing me to get an extended rider on the policy. Aches and pains aside, Sunbury is another town worth revisiting to absorb the local history and staying at the old Inn looks like a possible weekend bucket list activity.

Leaving Sunbury and traveling down Old 3C Road, I came to the small town of Galena where my map and compass skills were again challenged. A poorly placed sign on the road suggested a false left-hand turn onto the bike path that resulted in a five-mile departure from my intended route. Unfortunately, this detour included some significant hill work from which I would have to recover at a later time. Luckily, a fellow cyclist helped me regain my bearings and find my way back to Galena. Being familiar with the route, he mentioned that his local bike club was trying to improve the signage, allowing "through bikers" easier passage.

As the day progressed, the scenery started to change dramatically. The passage from the rural hills of Holmes County to the northwest corner of Columbus brought numerous strip malls, commercial businesses, and an increase in traffic. I had arrived in Dublin and the bike path had now turned back to city streets. As I had anticipated, the busyness of city life had become an agitation after two days of rural adventure. Despite regaining my sense of awareness for city traffic, numerous street changes made for tedious mapping through the urban geography. Under the midday sun and passing through a busy walkway, I came across an older lady on the opposite side of the street. She was nervously waiting for the signal to change so she could make her crossing.

Erma was local to Dublin and was on her way to the grocery store with her two-wheel cart. Out of general curiosity for each other, we struck up a warm conversation at this busy intersection. She was a 76-year-old widow who wore a pair of oversized framed glasses. Comically, her eyes appeared much larger than normal. She had been enduring macular degeneration in both eyes for the past 10 years but her energy and enthusiasm for life gave me the impression that she was a teenager with a pass to skip school for the day. As she began asking about my trip it became comical to me that she only had one temple on her glasses. Because of this, her glasses kept slipping down her face as we talked. I interrupted our discussion midstream to show her that I was perplexed with the same problem, as I had been sporting around with the same one-armed condition on my 2.0

readers. Together, we laughed at our situation and how silly we looked as well as the fact that we were determined to live with the condition rather than buy replacement glasses. As we talked, it was obvious that Erma needed to get on with her chores for the day. Being an old Eagle Scout, I offered to take her across the street. She graciously accepted so I laid my bike down and escorted her across. We exchanged best wishes on the other side of the street and, with that, we were each back on our own.

This type of exchange between total strangers has recurred numerous times throughout my travels and serves as a reminder that people are genuinely approachable and that the circumstances of life bring open participants together in the most unlikely times and places. This exchange with Erma and the many others will remain with me as fond memories through the years.

Road Rule Number Seven: *Riding alone doesn't mean you're lonesome.*

Fellow cyclist Bob Howells once wrote, "When you travel as a group, you're viewed as a group. You're assumed to be collectively self-sufficient. When you're alone, others see you as a fellow human being. People readily share their humanity with you. The earth and the people within unfold in proportion to your openness to them. Each of us has travel preferences that may include solo riding, group riding, or even event riding. The solo option in cycling opens the door to new acquaintances that may change your way of thinking."

Road Rule number seven is not so much about riding alone as it is about knowing what you want from a ride and how to best achieve these desires. The seasoned traveler may be in search of a new destination such as an unexplored national park. The young adventurer may want to navigate across a trail with GPS and the athlete may want to pound out mega miles; like a hundred miles day. In the end, there is a personal reward for each type of cyclist whether in large groups or as a soloist. Determine your motivations for riding; pick the options that best suit your desired travel, and ride with purpose. The long miles in the saddle will teach you to appreciate your surroundings with all of your senses and challenge you to look into your soul.

Leaving Dublin and entering the Olentangy Trail park became a challenge as the trail maps required frequent turns and offered poor trail marking for the "through rider". The park itself was very scenic and would have been a nice place to have lunch were it not for the poor routing and resulting disorientation. Though I asked for directions a number of times, the locals were not able to help me out of my Olentangy dilemma. This brought to mind Road Rule Number Eight.

Road Rule Number Eight: Know where you are and where you want to be. When in doubt, use multiple maps including state, local or trail.

The obvious reaction to this road rule is to employ the use of a GPS unit. However, many have experienced regions where even the best electronic devices lose reception or experience a blackout. Whether the GPS is your primary or secondary tool for navigation, it is important to know your bearings and to know that you're maintaining the planned trajectory or direction. Learn about the areas through which you will be traveling. Use natural features in your surroundings to keep your bearings correct.

While on a bicycle and generally in congested or urban environments, the need for confirming location checks increases when compared to the speed of a backpacker. There will be numerous challenges for the cyclists attempting to navigate through the congestion of information and traffic. Common mistakes on the cycling road include missed turns, hidden street signs, route numbers for road names, detours, and even good intentions but wrong directions. Each of these challenges can have a potentially disastrous effect.

Many years ago in rural Faulkton, South Dakota, I took a turn on an old county road, thinking that I could avoid a strong easterly head wind and later return to my east heading when the wind died down. Though the Triple AAA state maps showed my location and where I ultimately wanted to be, it certainly did not show the conditions I was about to experience along the way. What started as a formal asphalt road deteriorated progressively to the condition of a trail and I soon found myself in a fool's bet. Each reduction in road quality was met with the optimism that this was a temporary degradation and that the traveling surface would surely return to asphalt in the next mile. Twenty miles later, my wheels sinking in loose soil and surrounded by corn stalks, I was barely able to see the rooftop of the next farmhouse. Having made a decision to cut my losses, I found a farmer who admired my effort to visit him and he redirected me back down the road I had just traveled. I did return to town in time for lunch after a 40-mile mistake, a much humbled and wiser rider.

So the point of this Road Rule is to use all of the available resources—maps, local people, and GPS. Keep yourself informed to the largest extent possible as to where you are and where you want to be.

Regardless of the environment, it is easy to get turned around without perspective. For those without elaborate GPS-equipped bikes (like mine), the challenge is to maintain a bird's eye view with a state map for a general heading. Compare that state map with a city map or a local street-level map for details and possible directional cues. Even with these maps in hand, The Olentangy Park made me feel like a mouse in a maze. A wise scoutmaster once told me that when you're lost–in the woods, in the city, and metaphorically in life–it is most important to "know where you are and where you want to be". These are the first steps to recovery and have always served as good advice.

It took some time to break out of this perpetual do-loop (a common term used by my IT friends to describe an unending and inescapable path). Finally, after passing over the Olentangy River and bridge multiple times in heavy traffic, I discovered the obvious and yet obscure sign that allowed me to return to the bike trail.

After breaking out of the park, I began to see familiar sights of The Ohio State University. The towers of campus housing and, of course, the football stadium stood out on the horizon line. Passing through the OSU campus, I chose not to spend much time as it was summer break and the campus was a virtual ghost town. Traveling through the city traffic for the past few hours, my attitude about Columbus was not in a good place. In this area, the Olentangy River merges with the Scioto River under a maze of expressway bridges. The challenge of routing through Columbus on the southwest side continued as the path was more of a four-lane freeway than a conventional bike path. The directing signage was poor and routing ultimately led to Route 40, otherwise known as Broad Street. This was a dangerous passage and involved more risk than I would advise for even a seasoned road rider.

Finally, after a few miles on Route 40 (sidewalks notwithstanding), I made the crossing and was heading out of Columbus towards London. The trail quickly returned to a flat, rural farmland. The city street navigation was replaced by long, open stretches of bike path cutting through a vast expanse of cornfields. With the mid-afternoon sun bearing down on the path, the radiant heat was noticeable but not unbearable. The lost time and associated frustration in Columbus was turned into a positive energy that resulted in a higher pedaling cadence. Positioning my hands in the lower handlebar drops with my head down, I built up a head of steam that resulted in an 18-mile-an-hour pace, which I was able to continue for the next ten miles.

Arriving in London, the bike path merged seamlessly into the suburban streets. I was ready to put down stakes just about anywhere in town after an emotionally exhausting day. Just as my thoughts about the day's ride were winding down, I rode past a quaint bed and breakfast. I thought this would be a nice change of pace after sleeping poorly under the stars for the past couple of nights. If nothing else, at least a backyard spot with a garden hose would suffice and improve my overall disposition. Unfortunately, no one answered when I knocked and so I dismissed any thought of a restful night's sleep.

Collecting myself after this false hope, I returned to the bike and noticed the speedometer was showing 95 miles for the day. Staring back at the 95 miles made me feel as if the speedometer was taunting me to break the century mark of 100 miles for the day. The term "century" is a cyclist's shorthand reference for a good day's cycling effort. The century rider gets the same sort of satisfaction from the completion of this effort as a marathoner does in crossing the finish line at the end of a 26.2 mile run. Achieving this distance is uncommon, especially while carrying an additional load of supplies. Somewhere in this day, I was going to hit 100 miles even if it meant circling around town a couple of times.

I settled in on dinner at a local pizzeria for rest and refuel. Downing the carbohydrates had an effect similar to jet fuel for this engine of motion. A large pizza and a couple of lemonade drinks later, I felt rejuvenated to the point of pursuing a few more miles and achieving that elusive century mark. Before picking up my gear, the pizza shop staff asked where I was headed. They warned me not to camp too close to Xenia. "You don't want to be there", they said. Knowing the town of Xenia from years of running races there, I wrote this warning off as a crosstown rivalry. Back in the saddle with a belly full of pizza, I returned to the familiar churning of the pedals toward South Charleston.

A few miles further down the path of endless cornfields, I got off my bike and gave a primal victory shout for hitting the 100-mile mark. Of course, other than the birds, no one was in the vicinity to care. I took a celebratory picture of the speedometer as it turned over to 100 miles–a big deal for a rider with a loaded bike.

Road Rule Number Nine: Embrace your eccentricity. Everyone has one. Your mission is to find out what yours is.

It is truly an enlightening sensation to wake up every day in the outdoors with only one purpose–to find out what the day has in store for you. Some days are packed full of stimulation and others are... well... just plain boring. They could be flat, hot, and lacking companionship or they could be just a long, long grind. To the untrained mind, this can be pure torture and, quite honestly, the reason why endurance sport has a bad rap.

When in a rut, I have found a couple of practices to help break up the tedium of long distance riding. The first practice is something I label as associative thinking. Creating a hyper interest and curiosity in every facet of the ride leads to a more efficient performance but also breaks the monotony. Questions that come to mind include monitoring my cadence, miles, speed, ease of breathing, or the distance to the next grocery store. In the meantime, the miles melt away.

The other technique used is known as dissociative thinking. This requires a little creative courage but is equally effective at curing boredom. Your mind is a wonderful tool that can launch a thousand thoughts and emotions from poetic verse to favorite song lyric or a charming line from a movie. When alone on the long, desolate road, you can conjure any rock star you want to be. Go ahead and belt out a couple of favorite tunes. So what if you're off key or miss a word or two. It's the emotion from deep inside tied with the song that brings a rush of feelings. Though I risk dating myself, you may be surprised what comes from your soul, lying just beneath your boredom—possibly a Bob Seger tune or a line from Monty Python and the Holy Grail. For the intellectuals, it could be reciting the Gettysburg Address. Unless you're a karaoke regular, I recommend making sure there's plenty of space between you and anyone in earshot.

When touring, it's helpful to know what gets you excited each day. What are the limits of your personal comfort and to what extreme will you push your boundaries to get a rise out of the day? They are hard to find and sometimes difficult to separate from the mundane. When you find one, proclaim it as yours. Enjoy the small victories in life.

The peddling was much easier after a crowning century day. I started to look in earnest for a place to bed down. As I rolled past a trailer home along the path, I noticed a group of folks who were gathered in their reclining chairs around a cinderblock fire pit. They appeared to be three sheets to the wind. There were numerous junk cars littering the lot and since it just didn't look like the type of gathering I would hang with, I casually passed by with a wave of the hand. The scene gradually came together as I noticed, off in the distance a good 200 yards from the bike path, a large, two-bay garage with an awful, gut-wrenching noise coming from within. Clearly, the parents were off at a safe distance from their kids' struggling attempt at forming a grunge rock band. The guttural screaming along with an over-amplified guitarist and drummer was just enough to drive any inhabitant from their home. I was amazed at how far down the path I had to travel before out-distancing the grunge noise. Some one-half to three-quarters of a mile later, the guitar sound was no longer audible and the thumping beat of the drum was no longer piercing the otherwise calm, midwestern evening. It was time to bed down for the night.

With my tent set-up along the bike path and no one in sight in either direction of the path, I watched the sun set over the ocean of corn. With the sun not entirely settled beyond the horizon, it felt odd to lay down with unused daylight at 9:00 in the evening. With a 105-mile day behind me, and Cincinnati another 80 miles to the southwest, it was conceivable to think I could reach Cincinnati by nightfall the next day. By plan, my son (a second-year student at the University of Cincinnati) was waiting to receive me for a short time. As I drifted off to sleep, the thought of contacting Sean without a working phone was troubling. I would need to be creative the following day in order to make a connection.

Captains of Industry

Hope Memorial Bridge
Cleveland, OH

Heron in the Erie Canal
Independence, OH

Erie Canal Towpath (crushed limestone)
Independence, OH

Boston Store Visitor Center
Peninsula, OH

A thin white line

Lilly Pads
Akron, OH

Equipment Check
Akron, OH

Monument to Native American Carrying Canoe
Akron, OH

Lock Number 4
Canal Fulton, OH

Long Boat Crew
Canal Fulton, OH

Co-use Trail
Fredericksburg, OH

Bigfoot Statue
Killbuck, OH

Killbuck Train Station
Killbuck, OH

Clouds of Ohio
Gambier, OH

Bridges of Dreams
Brinkhaven, OH

Pennsylvania Railroad, Kokosing Gap Trail
Gambier, OH

Daniel Boone Knife
Xenia, OH

John A. Roebling Bridge
Cincinnati, OH

Graffiti
Riverside, OH

Camping
Outside of Xenia, OH

1905 Wright Flyer in Flight
Dayton, OH

Site of First NFL Game
Dayton, OH

Great Miami Bikeway
Tipp City, OH

A Path Through Ohio
Cleveland to Cincinnati to Xenia to Piqua

Day Four

Friday, July 18
South Charleston to Cincinnati - 95 Miles

While packing up in preparation for the next leg of my trip, I discovered stowaway passengers from the night before. It appears that the wheat field in which I slept was a perfect place for garden-variety slugs to be attracted to my body heat. At least a half dozen of the slimy critters were folded, pressed, and dried out from the pressure of my tightly wound tent. Others had surprisingly survived yesterday's long ride. In either case, they are a mess to deal with, sticking to everything outside the tent. The birds were rather talkative this morning as they quarreled back and forth without a care for my presence. The thicket in which they chose to hide made it difficult to see into as I tried to find the cause of the commotion. My guess is that the likely offenders were a couple of grouse or possibly our state bird, the cardinal.

The wheels were rolling by 6 am with the early morning sunrays on the path indicating another nice day ahead. However, looming in the distant northern sky behind me was a familiar red sky glowing through the underbelly of the low, moisture-bearing clouds. The polar vortex had made this trip nearly perfect with temperatures averaging 78 degrees and little humidity. With an old reference in mind–"red sky in morning, sailors take warning"–the threat of rain appeared imminent.

At this point, I was reminded of Road Rule Number Six; let go of your electronics. Even though I was trying to keep my cellphone charged for reports of my progress back to my wife, I was trying to not otherwise rely on my phone. This meant I had to read the signs provided by Mother Nature which I knew could prepare me for imminent weather challenges and would allow me the opportunity to find cover from severe weather, all without electronics.

The early mornings have been cool and dark requiring warm weather gear to start. My favorite articles of clothing include a winter hat and gloves, my trusty leg warmers (a holdover from my '83 cross-country trip), tights, baggy bike shorts, and a yellow windbreaker. This unconventional look, uniquely Looney and bordering on Bohemian, was layered in a way that allowed items to be easily stripped off when temperatures start to warm up.

My song of the day came in two parts. First was the 1978 classic by Kenny Rogers, "*The Gambler*"– *You got to know when to hold 'em, know when to show 'em*. The second, equally memorable song later became the choice for my morning karaoke with no care for harmony or lyric accuracy. It just felt good to belt out a couple of chords of "You've Lost That Loving Feeling", the 1980 version by Hall and Oates, (no disrespect for the earlier Righteous Brothers version from the '60s). Thankfully, there were no other humans along the path to see or hear this spectacle.

The next five miles on the way to Cedarville were rather uncomfortable as my undercarriage was feeling a bit sensitive, no doubt due to the earlier 100-mile day. A constant shifting in the saddle and a healthy dose of a popular diaper rash cream was required in order to get through the discomfort. However, after another 50 miles down the road, the memory of distress in this area would mash together anyway.

For the first time in the trip, a coffee shop presented itself at the time of need. This was going to be a good day. Generally, when getting on the road early, breakfast is a handful of nuts, dried fruit, and leftover Gatorade from the day before. God forbid there would be a repeat of that nasty breakfast drink from a couple days earlier. Entering Cedarville, the morning sun was beaming down on the main street of this small, out-of-session college town. The sun's rays cast their orange glow on the Bean and Cream coffee shop. Was this a dream? All that was missing was angels and harp music. On my first pass at 6:30, the shop appeared closed but I spied one customer inside and decided to make an entry.

I tied my trusted 85-pound loaded steel donkey to a bike rack out front. There's no need to lock it up in a town where the college student body won't be rolling over for several more hours. Having an unlimited choice of seating in the shop, I selected a window table and purchased a large coffee, muffin, and smoothie, good enough for round one. As the first infusion of caffeine coursed its way through my veins, the subtle warming effect of the coffee prepared me for catching up on my journal notes. Minutes later, a steady stream of people began to pour in and a buzz of the day's activities filled the air.

As I made my second trip to the counter, a burly patron shouted out, "Hey, I haven't seen leg warmers like those in years". The shop went silent waiting for my reaction. I replied proudly that I was the original owner of these 30-year-old, scrunchy leg warmers and I was sure Irene Cara would be happy to sell him her other pair on eBay. Of course, you would have to be a student of the 1980's movie, *Flashdance*, to get the reference. We both laughed at my functional but outdated apparel and we seized the opportunity to talk about how the bike path has brought outsiders to Cedarville. We went on for a while before I returned to writing, realizing that I eventually needed to get some miles in.

After a hearty breakfast, I got back on the bike and resumed my ride. Xenia came about quicker than expected. The city name originates from the Greek word for hospitality and I noticed the city's welcoming vibe as I passed through Shawnee Park. This is a city of many surprises with numerous bike trails radiating from the train depot. Because of this, Xenia has earned the nickname of "The Bicycle Capital of the Midwest". Xenia, and the larger Greene County, is also an area of important historical significance and the source of my intrigue for many years.

As I embarked on this cross-state journey, I was determined to spend time actually reading the state historical markers that are commonly found along the roadside. So many times in the past, during business or pleasure travel, I casually drove by, thinking to myself what might have happened in this area but never taking the time to get out and explore. In the planning stages of this ride across Ohio, I committed myself to stop, photograph, and read each state marker that was within sight of the trail. Deep within the description of each marker was a local point of interest, a person of note, or an event that occurred in the general vicinity of the marker. At a bicyclist's pace, this was the perfect time to explore the deeper meaning and historical significance described on the marker that helped shaped the state. A full listing of each marker found en route is provided in the appendix.

Having lived near Xenia for a number of years, I had come to know of its historical importance and was quite certain I would find much more while riding on a bike at a slower pace. In this regard, Xenia certainly did not disappoint. As an aspiring adventurer, I had read many books about the noteworthy pioneers of the early 18th century. Their stories of pursuit and conquest had left a trail of curiosity for me to rediscover. On my bucket list was my desire to become more acquainted with my boyhood heroes, famous pioneers Daniel Boone and Simon Kenton. As it turned out, Xenia was a significant crossing territory for both as they traveled up and down the Ohio River Valley and into Kentucky for seasonal hunting.

To my surprise, Xenia boasted a sizable historical center known as the Greene County Historical Society, which claims possession to numerous artifacts of this early American lifestyle. This was an opportune time for me to reacquaint myself with this region's history. While waiting for the museum to open in the morning, I took the opportunity to walk around a nearby reconstructed, two-story log cabin. I admired the careful dovetailing of the logs at its corners and the white contrasting mortar used as fill for the aged cracks between each member. The wafting aroma of the well-maintained herb garden framed by a stone walkway gave an ambiance of a well thought-out existence and sense of permanence.

Returning promptly at 10 o'clock, I met with the historical society's director, Catherine Wilson, at the door and commented on the beautiful restoration of the log cabin out front. We talked for a while as I explained the purpose of my visit with a specific interest in Simon Kenton and Daniel Boone's history. Catherine was nice enough to give me a personalized tour and started the conversation with her lifelong residence in Xenia and her distant familial connection to Daniel Boone. I thought to myself, well, if you're going to discuss history why not discuss it with a family member. From the center room, Catherine was able to point to different sections of the two-floor gallery and described the area I had the most interest in–the early pioneer section.

Through an earlier Internet search, I learned that the Xenia museum had housed the flintlock rifle used by Simon Kenton. Actually seeing this relic became one of the latest additions to my bucket list. Having read a great deal about Kenton's marksmanship and legendary skill with the gun, I had built a Christmas morning-like anticipation to seeing the actual article. I tried to contain my enthusiasm for seeing the gun as Catherine went on about Xenia's history. Finally, unable to contain my curiosity any longer, I asked if she knew anything about the Kenton rifle. Despite the fact that I may have used my outside voice a bit too much, she kindly replied, "Oh, but of course. It's in my office". We made our way to her office, which was just a few steps from where we were standing. The gun, housed in its own deep frame, was hanging over her desk. For an old Kenton fan, it was like finding a lost puzzle piece and filling the final hole in the picture. Very satisfying.

To my surprise, just below the rifle hung another deep frame that housed a primitive jackknife, half opened to display the blade. The entirety of the knife was eight inches in length. On the handle was an inscription; DBOON. Indeed, I was looking at another piece of history, this one carried by the great Daniel Boone. Catherine described how the gun and knife were received as a gift through the James Galloway family. Galloway had been an early resident of Greene County and the builder of the admirable, early 1800s era cabin that sat in front of the museum. Galloway had befriended both Kenton and Boone as a matter of survival while mapping early Greene County. After having taken a few pictures of the gun and knife, we both took a walk to the Galloway cabin where the articles had been housed originally. As we crossed through the herb garden, I had to ask Catherine why the gun was on display in her office. Surely, a relic such as this deserves a prominent home in the center of the museum. Catherine responded that, subsequent to an incident a few years back, they like to keep it under multiple security systems.

Walking through the Galloway cabin, Catherine described that the structure had been moved three times before making its way to its present location. She added that it had also seen a number of restorations and presently contained about 70% of its original logs. I learned that Galloway was one of the first settlers of the area and started the early survey work for what is now known as Greene County. As Catherine described Galloway's history, I envisioned this simple two-floor structure becoming a secure meeting point for early pioneers to exchange tales of their travels and tribulations during a rather untamed and downright dangerous time for early settlers.

On the way back to the museum, Catherine became more relaxed as we realized that we had many periods of common historical interest. Possibly pushing the "too inquisitive" side of every conversation, I found Catherine's occupation as the proprietor of a small museum rather intriguing. Catherine not only had an interest in the local history but was also an actual part in this history as she described another monumental event in Xenia's past. The year was 1974 and, as a young girl of nine, she and her siblings were quickly rushed to the family bathtub as a dark and ominous cloud gathered. What happened in the next half hour resulted in the razing of the city of Xenia. Being at the tail end of tornado alley, Xenia was not accustomed to tornados or certainly what was to happen next. On this particular April day, a category F5 tornado struck Xenia, killing 33 and injuring 1,300 more. Fortunately for Catherine and her family, they all survived. In the years to follow, a sense of obligation to family and local history lead her to become a knowledgeable source of local history and a natural representative of the Xenia and Greene County Historical Society.

I had spent more time than I had planned and felt the need to get back on the road again. I told Catherine that I enjoyed every minute of our discussion. In turn, she asked me if I would sign her visitor log and let everyone with whom I come into contact know about this gem of a spot along the Ohio to Erie Bike trail. Without a doubt, she had my commitment.

Remembering that my cell phone drained its power on the first day of the ride, I had been out of touch with my family for most of the week. Adding insult to injury, I had grabbed the wrong power cord and was unable to charge the phone anyway. Too frugal and too frustrated with the durability of my electronic equipment, I asked Catherine if I could make one telephone call on her landline. Of course, in a museum with marginal funding, the call was on a vintage 1980's style phone; a museum relic in its own right compared to today's technology.

The call to my wife of 26 years went as expected.

Road Rule Number Ten: Always leave a trail of where you've been and where you're going.

In the 2000s, a book titled Between a Rock and a Hard Place written by adventurer Aron Ralston describes his survival experience on a rock-climbing trip in Blue John Canyon in Utah. In the course of his trip, his arm became pinched between a sizable rock formation and a large boulder. Ralston found himself unable to extricate his arm from between the two surfaces. Even worse, he was stuck with limited supplies. The following six days became a gripping tale of survival. Aron later admitted that the whole ordeal could have been avoided if he had just let someone know where he was going and how long he planned to be out of town.

The point here is to keep in touch with someone while striking out on a new adventure. Self-reliance is important for all adventurers but an ounce of preparation such as a compiling a travel itinerary or carrying a charged cell phone can save your hide from the unexpected. By the way, I recommend the book, especially if you're an adrenaline junkie.

———————————————◦———————————————

When on the road alone, it is important to keep your loved ones informed about your movements in the unlikely but altogether possible event that something goes wrong. To my credit, I left a financial trail with the credit card that I had used to purchase food in each town. Though we had not spoken, I knew that Laurie's nature as a financial hawk when it comes to credit card spending meant that she was generally aware of my location. As for my personal well-being, I had been out of touch for three days and I anticipated that Laurie was fuming over my "off the radar" communication style. True to form, my opening explanation did not justify my lack of communication and I received my due correction. As the call wrapped up, I left word that Cincinnati was within striking distance by the end of the day. I pictured a relatively easy 60-mile ride into Cincinnati where my son, Sean was attending college. I could envision pushing back a couple beers and grabbing a hot shower as Sean and I burned the late hours.

Boy, I couldn't have been more wrong about this projection.

Once I had finished my phone call home, I prepared to head back out on the road but before doing so, I asked Catherine one final question. I was curious about the issue with the Simon Kenton gun. She told me that the gun had gone missing in the early 70s, just before the '74 tornado. The building that originally housed the rifle was demolished along with many other artifacts during the storm. A dozen or so years later, a mysterious call was received from Texas in which the caller asked if the museum was missing an antique muzzleloader. The caller mentioned the Xenia Historical Center property tag, which marked the gun and thought the gun had some historical value. Soon after, the gun was returned to its rightful owner and put back on display to be shared with the general public. This little footnote of history made the visit even more compelling and well worth the effort of making a stop.

The next part of the day should have been an easy, flat, 60-mile day as I traced the Little Miami River into Cincinnati where it gently flows into the Ohio River. The reconstructed Xenia train depot now served as the hub of Ohio's bike network, sending riders and pedestrians off in many directions as the paths radiate from the hub. With map in hand and studying my route toward Cincinnati, I chose an incorrect trail marker.

Despite my best efforts to pick the correct trail, the route I chose sent me–incorrectly–northwest towards Yellow Springs rather than south to Cincinnati. Little did I know that the day's difficulties were just beginning as I purposefully headed out of Xenia in the wrong direction.

Many miles later on the bike trail, I came across a runner who appeared to be having dehydration issues and was cramping and dry heaving on the side of the path. I stopped to offer her some consolation and water. With two full water bottles carried on the bike frame, I offered the first bottle. The runner was appreciative for the water and the recognition of her situation. She claimed I was an angel in disguise. I had to think twice about this knowing I had been three days on a bike and was pretty pungent smelling for an angel. We continued exchanging running snippets and then she asked where I was heading. I boldly claimed, "Cincinnati" and told her I was planning to arrive that evening. I was dumbstruck when she pointed out on my map that I was heading in the wrong direction. If I continued much further, I would make Springfield, placing me 20 miles in the wrong direction. At this point, I was feeling pretty humiliated and frustrated with my obvious error. Thankfully, this total stranger had saved me from a worse loss of time. I was now feeling like an angel had been sent my way. This little exchange brings to mind the importance of the next road rule.

Road Rule Number Eleven: Be an ambassador for cycling and be nice to strangers.

In other parts of the world where nomadic travel is a way of life, the traveler is an emissary carrying a message of peace or care for one family or another. In eastern Africa, an old Swahili proverb is commonly used to describe the role of the traveler; "Mgeni aje mwenyeji apone". This roughly translates to "When the guest visits, the host is healed". Many miles of travel have exposed me to those with a dream to be untethered from their life conditions, much as a touring cyclist is untethered from the office chair or work routine. As cyclists, we carry a rare trait of optimism no matter the condition. Yes, we can complain with the best of them but when it comes to enduring distress or physical hardship, the cyclist is equipped like no other. The optimism of the next sunny day, the next farmer's market (and the opportunity to gorge on food), or the next downhill cruise is always around the next corner and often are the stuff of which food dreams are made. With this positive outlook on life, the cycling tourist has a rare opportunity to influence others to experience their surroundings beyond the comfort of a car. The cycling tourist is an ambassador who awakens the possibility that a ride around the block, a ride to the next neighborhood, or a ride across town is achievable. Distant cycling at its core increases the confidence to be self-reliant and go the next mile. Many years ago while riding through a small farming town in rural Wisconsin, I was coming to the end of a long day with my heavy load on two wheels. I was suddenly startled by a young boy who snuck up behind me on his Stingray bike. He was curious enough to ask, "Where ya going, mister?" As I explained my mission of riding through not just his state but many others as well, he blurted back that he wanted to do that some day. As the chitchat continued over the next couple of miles, we were as close as two kids dreaming about the future from the end of an old, wooden fishing pier. Shortly thereafter, he sped away. Some distance later, I found his bike on the side of the road. The boy and his family were nearby, out in front of their family farm and grocery. As I passed, they waved me down from their front porch and insisted that I select some fresh fruit and cheese from their grocery. This was a small but welcome bonanza for a calorie-craved cyclist. As I walked away from the barn, a faded sign advertising Colby Cheese caught my eye. As I packed up my bike with cheese, I could not help but wonder if this was part of the famed Colby Cheese family.

I don't know if the young rider ever took his Stingray cycling aspirations beyond the family farm but I do know he learned about dreaming big that day.

I was fifteen miles out of Xenia and headed in the wrong direction! I quickly reversed my heading on the path and reassessed my situation. A visit with my son would now take a near heroic effort. Instead of a relaxed 67-mile day, I was looking at a 100-plus mile day. Furthermore, was this middle-aged body physically capable of turning back-to-back centuries? From within, a familiar feeling emerged best described as a controlled rage. The competitor inside immediately woke up for the challenge.

Game on.

With ear buds plugged in and riding in the lower portion of the handlebars, known as the "drops", I returned to Xenia by 12:30 averaging 15-miles-per-hour while carrying an 85-pound load. The self-talk along the way was a mix of internal criticism and a rolling calculation factored to achieve the goal of arriving in Cincinnati by nightfall. This was going to be a clear example of brawn over brains that had gotten me out of jams in the past. Stopping at a roadside Subway, I grabbed a tuna foot-long and devoured each section of the sandwich while jamming to some IPod tunes. It was a literal "eat and ride".

Back in Xenia, I came across a group of riders all colorfully dressed in bike jerseys and participating in a   multi-day bike tour that was occurring over the weekend. According to the markings on the path, there appeared to be options of 30, 60, and 100-mile rides each, all originating in Xenia. As I was now crossing paths with the returning groups dressed in their polyester event tech shirts designed to commemorate the event, I grinned at my fashion-challenged appearance. Funnier yet were the pieces of lettuce and tuna from the submarine sandwich that had been splattered on my t-shirt while I was eating on the ride. The returning cyclists reminded me of a curiosity of human nature that occurred to me when I was a runner. The challenge is an old social experiment testing the friendly jesters of a total stranger performing the same activity in an opposing direction. While on the road with a steady stream of oncoming cyclists, I had the opportunity to apply some statistical science to the question of whether or not two strangers who are passing one another while traveling in opposite directions will acknowledge or wave to one another. My inference was that the two strangers would likely not greet each other.

As I continued to wave at each rider, I took note of the mixed reaction from the 100 or so riders that passed. The responses ranged from a nod of the head to a returned hand gesture to a "stare straight ahead and ignore the crazy old dude with a four-day growth of beard and an unkempt appearance" type of response. Many riders were wearing headphones and I found the reactions of those riders interesting and similar to the reactions of those in the running community. It was about a 30/30/30 split of acknowledgment including the wave, the verbal, and the snub. This would make an interesting Ph.D. study considering the demographics and environmental variations. Meanwhile, the streaming hodgepodge of bike equipment continued, including hybrids, tandems, faring-equipped, recumbent, and road bikes.

As my days ride continued through the Miami Valley, signs for the future site of the Fort Ancient Museum appeared along the trail. This site had largely been an attraction featuring the early Paleo-Ohio civilizations. The Hopewell Indian tribe had ruled up and down the Little Miami River for centuries before European interests began to develop in the east. These tribes occupied the region between 200 BC and 300 AD and found the area plentiful for nourishment and for ease of transportation. After some hard bike miles, I decided to take a side excursion on foot to see this historic site. A small sign on the path gave the impression that a short quarter-mile walk would place me at the ancient site. The short distance became a major undertaking as the uphill climb was on an undeveloped path. My hard-soled bike shoes did not make the task any easier as I struggled to gain traction on my way up the hill.

Finally on the top and at first glance, Fort Ancient appeared to be a large football field with mounding hills around its perimeter. As I studied the mounds in the open grassy space, I started to make sense of the layout and organization. A quick read of the historical placards tells of a scientific change of thought in which the mounds, originally thought to be some manner of fortification, are now thought to be a large-scale sundial or a modern day calendar, similar in purpose to England's Stonehenge.

The return trip down the steep embankment proved equally treacherous in my hard-soled shoes as I navigated back through the trail with natural obstacles and loose shale. The descent was complicated as a light drizzle, which had been falling since Xenia, was now turning to rain accompanied by heavy, dark clouds. Returning to my bike, I decided to pedal on as the canopy of trees softened the constant rain. As I made my way, the wind-driven rain became a steady downpour and forced me to pull out my rain gear. Slipping on the bright yellow gear allowed my core body temperature to regulate in spite of the rain and provided a shallow sense of security.

Oftentimes when alone on the road and with the elements working against me, even a shadow of negativity can dramatically affect my ability to physically and intellectually deal with the real or perceived situation. An old hiker once told me, "As the mind goes so does the body". When faced with these situations, I find it important to maintain a realistically positive perspective of my situation. Once again, an old, favorite song to break the cycle of negative thoughts is in order. In this case, my song of choice was an old REO Speedwagon song, "Keep Pushin". I followed this musical reverie with a near clinical assessment of my condition:

Food? - Check.
Core temperature? - Check.

Fluids? - Check.
Remaining strength? - Check.

Finally, I assessed my environment and equipment. If I can rationally work through these thoughts, I am generally moving in the right direction.

Road Rule Number Twelve: Stop the negative, replace with positive and realistically assess.

When working with the Boy Scouts as a troop leader, we often ended our long days by sitting around a campfire ring and sharing our thoughts about the day's strenuous hike or other events. This exercise was commonly known as "thorns, rose, and buds ". In turn, each scout would reflect on his likes, dislikes, and most importantly the opportunities that each hoped to see, do, or achieve in the coming days. Surprisingly, even on the most strenuous of days and in the most inclement conditions, each scout could dig deep enough to find one ember of hope that would keep him motivated to move forward. When performing most physical activities, your mind is assessing your body and its performance. On a surface level, it may be a sore knee or a nagging hitch in a running stride. Each of the day's little events or environmental conditions are also continually being assessed and creating a disposition that can range from euphoric and positive to brooding and negative. Whatever the condition, it is important to be in tune with these changes in mood and outlook.

To stay realistically positive is to recognize the negative elements causing your poor outlook and objectively identify a positive outcome with your available skills and resources. Even when your immediate future looks gloomy, assess all of your skills, your resources, and your equipment when trying to determine a course of action that will lead you to a better outcome. Stay calm and generally unemotional. Think through your options, determine your corrections, and don't procrastinate in taking action.

It was now early evening and the odometer was reading 90 miles. The combination of rain, consecutive days of long miles, and now saddle soreness to the tender undercarriage forced a walk break every 10 miles or so, just to break up the monotony of pedaling. This was a particularly scenic part of the ride, passing through old whistle-stop towns such as Loveland. This charming, New England-type setting poised alongside the rail was at one time a popular bedroom community for the booming city of Cincinnati. A 30-minute commute by train made for a hassle-free portage into the city some 100 years ago. Now the town has been carefully transformed into a stop for bikers and other tourists looking for a glimpse of the "good old days".

Breaking up the ride into ten-mile segments allowed me enough rest and the chance to regain my determination to arrive in Cincinnati at a reasonable hour and in time to grab dinner with Sean. Finally, a familiar bridge crossing over the Little Miami River was in view. I knew from past rides that I was nearing the end of the trail. The path consistently kept the river to my right-hand side as I traveled south with the flow of the current. Suddenly, the river swept to the left under one bridge and back again under a different bridge and I knew that the Miami Valley Golf Club would soon be on my right.

As of this writing, The Ohio to Erie Bike Trail markers abruptly end at the golf course. Looking at my city maps, I saw that there was another dangerous stretch of four-lane road that allowed passage to the Ohio River. The now-dark five-mile route, the Friday night traffic, and a persistent rain made my next decision clear. I smartly decided to try to phone Sean from the Miami Valley golf pro's office. The pro was kind enough to let me into the shop to make a call. Within a half hour, Sean had picked me up and taken me back to his apartment on Calhoun Street in the Clifton neighborhood that was also the home of the University of Cincinnati. After a hot shower, dinner at Buffalo Wild Wings, and a couple beers, the negatives of the day were all but washed away. Over dinner, Sean and I agreed to meet at the local Starbucks the next morning since he worked the early shift at the golf course. I had worked the links for many years when I was his age so this was not only an interesting reversal of roles but also an agreeable way to end this leg of the Ohio to Erie Bike Trail.

After dinner, Sean and I walked back to his dorm room and called it a night. As the rain continued to beat against the windowpane, my last thought as my head hit the pillow was that I picked a good night to be inside rather than tenting in the rain. Such is the gamble of travel by bike.

Day Five

Saturday, July 19
Mount Liberty to South Charleston - 105 miles

Following our plan, Sean was off to an early start at the golf
course. As I was enjoying the day's first coffee at Starbucks
on Calhoun Street, I began jotting down the previous day's
activities in my journal. As the pedestrian traffic ambled by
the front window, this quiet time allowed me to get my
thoughts committed to paper. While I was deep in thought, a
curious young man casually approached and introduced
himself as Preston, a University of Cincinnati English major
who was teaching at a local high school. As a side vocation,
he also assisted inexperienced writers in composing and
editing their heart-felt journals of thought and intrigue into a
formal publication. As one example, he described a drug
addict who made good on his life after an unfortunate
beginning and a conversion to Christianity. Now a
productive contributor to society, this former drug addict is
working with at-risk inner-city kids to prevent the same
experiences from occurring in their lives. Preston described
numerous websites that could provide similar assistance in

composition and editing if a person was interested in such things.

I showed Preston the map of the Ohio to Erie Trail and he showed a genuine interest in the trip. This interest started my creative juices flowing about my adventure travels and my aspirations to publish the travel notes. We casually discussed the publishing process for a while and he left me with some ideas to ponder in the future. Though I never thought of myself as a writer, Preston's comments planted a seed that one-day might bear fruit. If you're reading this now in a formal publication, we can credit Preston for the motivation. Like Preston, many of the other people I've met during my travels bring to mind Road Rule Number 13. The casual and random acquaintances we make each day may redirect a destination or crystalize an inner passion.

Road Rule Number Thirteen: Meet someone interesting daily. Allow conversations to develop. These are the gems of the day.

When I first biked across the country as a young man, the bike and the travel became a vehicle for seeing national parks and recognizable sights. Looking back after 30-years of travel by bike, I realized that I missed a sizeable portion of self-discovery and purpose for the ride. Replaying the mental tape many years later, the memories that come back in full color are the people that I met and the impressions that they left on me. Don't get me wrong; the photographs and postcard images are all equally beautiful and serene but the brief acquaintances with other human beings carries an emotional context that remains etched in our memory for years afterward.

With many miles of cycle travel behind me, I have experienced highs and lows from each and what I have concluded to be the most memorable achievements are not the places I've been nor the miles I've ridden nor the pain I have endured. The memories most cherished are those that involve human contact and the brief exchange of ideas with people from different backgrounds.

———————————⟫○⟪———————————

It was at about this point that Sean joined Preston and me having returned from the golf course and we polished off a couple cups of coffee. By then, it was time for me to get back on the trail. I picked up my maps and wished Preston good luck with his endeavors. Sean and I were headed to the Ohio River for a ceremonial "wheel dip" of my steel donkey, a self-indulging and self-created ceremony of the southern state line crossing.

A short time later, Sean and I stood on the banks of the Ohio. We looked in both directions in an attempt to grasp the size of the great river. Across the river on the Kentucky side, we spied a vintage paddle wheel boat with its large, red wheel positioned at the rear of the boat. This was one of the earliest forms of motorized propulsion used to travel up and down these waterways. Originally powered by compressed steam, later models were powered by diesel engines, which served to turn the paddlewheel boat through the water. These relics from the late 1800s are used today to support a popular tourism trade in this region. A couple of boats could be seen unloading passengers on the Kentucky side. We continued to walk further along the river parkway toward the massive stanchions of the John Roebling Bridge. These impressive stanchions tower high above the river on both sides. The John Roebling Bridge is an early example of a suspension bridge designed by its namesake. Two massive buttresses made of local sandstone flank either side of the Ohio's edge and are connected by long spans of bundled cable.

The Roebling Bridge stands today, as one of the country's first suspension bridges. This iconic bridge was completed in 1866 as the first major connector between Ohio and Kentucky. At the time of completion, this was the world's longest suspension bridge, boasting a span of just over 1,000 feet in length. The bridge carries many similar features of its famous sister to the east, the Brooklyn Bridge, which was constructed by Roebling's son 30 years later. As we walked around the historic bridge, I reflected on the familial connection of these two historic bridges.

Having completed our short ceremony of dipping the steel donkey in the Ohio River, Sean agreed to take my bike and me back to Xenia, avoiding a retracing of yesterday's sprint down to Cincinnati. With a quick lunch and a man-hug, we parted ways, each heading in our own direction. The Xenia Train Depot was exactly the same as I had left it yesterday. I carefully read all my maps and took note of Road Rule

Number Six again; *Let go of the electronics, use your surroundings, and use your senses.*

I certainly did not want a repeat of yesterday's misdirection debacle. Heading northwest to Dayton, I picked up my route and got back on the path.

Despite yesterday's wet and raw finish, there were few complaints from the undercarriage department. I started to find the day's cadence and was feeling pretty good about a short day's effort ending in Troy. After 20 miles or so, I approached the Riverside - Linden Township line. The trail narrowed and took an unexpected hard right-hand turn but there was a lack of trail change markings. I took note of the turn and continued left in a southwest direction that appeared to be the main trail. Within a mile of this intersection, it became evident that I had incorrectly chosen my trail option. Unfortunately, my surroundings took a turn for the worse and did not pass the safety gut check–on a bicycle no less. I did not want to get lost in this area so I quickly whipped out the maps to regain my bearings. On the proverbial "other side of the tracks", indicators of danger lurked. Garbage caught in the nearby brush, broken bottles in the street, and the rank smell of urine lingering in the air all suggested neglect. On the path, I approached a middle-aged woman slowly churning the pedals of a rusty, old, single-speed Stingray bike. She was clearly oversized for the bike as she hunched over the handlebars with her knees nearly hitting her chin. As I came up from behind, I offered my traditional salutation. When she looked up at me I was aghast by her distressed face, almost in tears, with what looked to be a fresh black eye. Shocked by this sight, I squeaked out a meager offering of help as I assumed it was violence-related based on the general surroundings. I did not get much of a response as she continued to push the pedals and wanted no part of a conversation with me. I did not have a lot to offer other than water and possible empathy, not that I looked like an EMT or any other caregiver for that matter. She was clearly on a different planet and wanted no part of mine. I continued on, wondering how else I could reach her. All within a short mile of my ill-fated heading, I made my correction and started cycling back to the missed trail change. The distraught cyclist now was nowhere to be found as she had apparently disappeared into the gloomy fabric of neglect found in this rundown part of town. As I retraced my route, I passed some old factory buildings and found one bright spot amongst the scenes of dilapidation. Some rather gifted and colorful artists had turned an otherwise depressed area into a brilliant array of color and messaging on the surrounding buildings. Even though empty spray paint cans littered the ground, there was clearly talent in this graffiti. In fact, I felt some of the art was worthy of an exhibit at New York's Museum of Modern Art. Panel after panel of bold, colorful letters delivered a somewhat cryptic message, making little or no word sense that I could recognize.

With the general condition of the neighborhood and a new bike path cutting through this area, there is a hope that one day a positive light will shine on this neglected part of town. Clearly, the bike trail intends to cut across the fabric of Ohio. This often times takes in the natural beauty of the state and occasionally serves as a harsh reminder of the reality of poverty and neglect within not only our great state but our country as well. It is for these experiences that bike travel is enviable and is sometimes coupled with the responsibility to help improve what is wrong.

Having lived in the Dayton area, I took the opportunity to see some of the sights of a recently re-imagined waterfront park along the Great Miami River. This park includes water fountains, gardens, and bike paths. Additionally, a number of memorials honoring two of Dayton's favorite inventors, Wilbur and Orville Wright commemorate their achievements within sight of the bike path. The path conveniently follows the Mad River into the city and crosses under a pedestrian bridge that takes a northern tack along the Little Miami River.

Taking a divergent trail from the north-south passage along the Great Miami allows one to view numerous historic landmarks made famous by the brothers back in the early 1900s. My trip was not complete without a quick stop on the west side of Dayton and the site of the original bike shop used by Wilber and Orville which doubled as the first working airplane shop. A block away was the foundation of their family home. With Ohio's license plate boasting "The Birthplace of Aviation", Dayton is surely its epicenter.

As a quick historical footnote, the title of "aviation's birthplace" is commonly contested by North Carolina. With its Atlantic coast location and constant wind, the North Carolina city of Kitty Hawk was the location where the brothers first lifted into the sky in their heavier-than-air flying machine and into history. With available time, a side trip is worth the effort to visit the Wright Brother's Dayton home and shop as well as the Wright - Patterson Air Force Base and Museum, which memorializes the many advances in aviation that have been made in the past one hundred years.

As I returned to the north-south branch of the bike trail in Dayton, I passed one of a number of circular concrete abutments about eight feet in diameter. The towering metal structures atop each footing point skyward. Each of these commemorates Dayton's recovery from the Great Flood of 1913. The haunting memory of the New Orleans flood in 2005 quickly comes to mind when recalling Dayton's tragic early twentieth-century event. The city's precarious location within the Miami River floodplain with its marginal levees became the Achilles' heel for this budding industrial city. A late-night March storm and the convergence of four separate river systems into the Great Miami River resulted in 20 feet of water flooding the city's main streets by 1:30 am the next day. Three hundred people in Dayton alone lost their lives as the chilly snow's melt grabbed any structure within its path and breached the existing embankments.

In the wake of this epic flood and $100 million dollars in damage–two billion in today's dollars–Ohio's Governor James Cox vowed that the city would never flood again and created one of the nation's first flood control programs and commission. Traveling north, an extensive network of levees, storage basins, and dams have been created and designed to channel excess water. A short journey north from Dayton will take riders over the Englewood Dam, creating the steepest climb for the day and a prime example of the enormity of this undertaking.

Following the Great Miami north, the bike path meanders alongside a gentler pace of water flow. Through the trees that line the river, another causality of the Great Flood can be seen and is commemorated with a historic marker along the bike path. The Town of Tadmor, a once vibrant whistle-stop town, was literally wiped off the map during the flood of 1913. Remnants of old bridge foundations, pathways, and building blocks of houses can been seen a short distance from the path. It's just another painful reminder of Mother Nature's fury, frozen in a time when horse path, canal, and train served this budding community a hundred years earlier. Tadmor is now just a Midwest version of a vacant ghost town.

The bike path continues to parallel the Erie Canal system providing a historical reminder of the prosperous cities alongside the canal. The communities of Tipp City, Troy, and Piqua each started as strategic outposts for early pioneers. The fertile soil of the Miami River Valley was recognized for its fruitful farming soil and it attracted more people from the east in search of their own livelihood. The emergent communities quickly outgrew their ability to sell and transport their goods to the northern great lakes and to the southern Ohio River. As with the eastern branch (circa. the 1820s), the western branches were opening up access to the western Ohio markets.

A canal boat once used for delivery service can be found on display along the path in Tipp City. Though the canals are overgrown, it is still possible to make out the channels carved by hard labor. The bike paths are likely traversing on the embankments once used as retaining walls for the water flowing through the canal. During the period of the big dig, these towns once served as home to hundreds of immigrant workers who dug the canals by hand. One observer documented that no less than 50 men in a row pushing wheelbarrows to the embankments of the canal could be seen from his perch. Small communities grew into larger ones as the development of canal, rail, and automotive travel quickly outpaced one another. It was now possible to transport produce from field to table in half the time and over increasingly longer distances. Improvement in transportation lowered product cost and increased the development of commerce along the western side of the state. By the mid-1830s, Ohio was the third most populous state in the country followed by New York and Pennsylvania, each of which was also building canals.

Troy is roughly five miles north of Tipp City along the bike path. In many locations, the Erie Canal and its feeder river, the Great Miami, border the bike path. This western branch was also known at the time as the Miami Canal in an effort to distinguish it from its eastern sister, the Ohio Canal. Along the path, a couple of great examples of lock chambers can be seen showing the finish stonework and joinery techniques of the times. Generally, these chambers were 90 feet in length and 15 feet in width and could accommodate a single boat measuring 85 feet by 14 feet. These long boats could carry up to 50 tons of cargo each. As each boat passed through the locks, a toll was sure to be collected. Many long boat operators traveled day and night with the crew and mules taking shifts.

As the path continues through Troy, a large, open field with a red barn at one end is home to the WACO (sounds like taco) airfield. This site boasts the first commercial aircraft runway with its production plants nearby. The Weaver Aircraft Company of Ohio got its start in 1919, soon after the Wright Brothers conquered the sky. The aircraft was a sturdy biplane, predominantly used by businessmen and the postal service. During World War II, the company converted their facilities to build gliders that were then notably used during the D-Day invasion of Normandy.

The path gently crosses back and forth over the river as it traverses through Troy. Soon, the city football stadium comes into view and is the present site for one of the oldest high school football rivalries in the country dating back to 1899 with rival high school, Piqua, to the north. This Midwest Friday night event has gone back and forth for, at last count, 130 times with each side boasting 62 wins each (and 6 ties). In full disclosure, Troy was home for our family and many of our friends still live just on the other side of the river from the stadium. If time allows, Troy is a great spot to grab a bite to eat and walk the friendly midwestern streets where today the town is known for its pleasant disposition and core family values.

Ten miles to the north of Troy sits another city of historical importance where westbound settlers and the indigenous Indian tribes of the area were commonly in conflict with one another. The city of Piqua, formerly known as Fort Piqua, (circa. 1747), became an early pioneer settlement along the Little Miami River. Because of its location along the popular trade route of the Miami River, the occupying British outpost found itself increasingly under attack by the Eastern Woodland Indian tribes. These skirmishes in Fort Piqua and other locations within the Miami Valley increased in intensity and later become part of what is now known as the Indian Wars. In the early 1800s, when the area was under American control, the government commissioned John Johnston as an Indian agent to this region.

While in this role, Johnston renewed relations between the warring factions of Indians and incumbent pioneers through cooperative trade and commerce. He built up the local agriculture while maintaining the peace in this prosperous western Ohio boundary town. Today, the legacy of Johnston's efforts as an agent, farmer, canal commissioner, and statesman can be observed at The Johnston Farm and Indian Agency Museum. This living museum and site of historical significance serves the community as a cultural reminder of its history in which a difficult past grew into a thriving community.

Today, Johnston's Farms serves as a significant gathering site for "Pioneer Days", bringing artisans of the older, skilled trades together for a reunion of this great era. In recent years, Piqua has also developed a network of bike paths, known as the Linear Loop Park. For many years, Piqua has embraced cyclists and pedestrians of many types to share in their history and enjoy life along the canals. With coffee as the primary motivator for this cyclist, I always recommend to other travelers I meet on the route to stop at Winan's Chocolates. They serve up a great beverage, hot or cold and, if you have more time, you can indulge in this third generation family delicacy (and my personal favorite), the seasonal chocolate-covered strawberries or Ohio's favorite, the buckeye. Trust me; don't worry about the calories. If you've made it this far on bike, you've earned a treat.

As of this writing, the north-south branch of the Miami Valley Bikeway finds its end in Piqua. The local and regional city commissions to the north are each working to secure property easements within city jurisdiction and, in time, are intent on connecting each. With travels through GOBA and other group rides, there many more cities to visit on the way north to Lake Erie. At the pace of a touring cyclist, each is open to exploration at the rider's desire. The people of Ohio, the history of Ohio, and the scenery of Ohio are each a study of dynamic change in their own right. Woven together, a patchwork of creative ingenuity, solid core values, hard work, and available resources, results in a quilt of midwestern values.

Nearing the day's end and feeling satisfied with the day's work, I decided to head back down the trail from which I came; back to Troy; a place I once called home. Knowing the wooded trails well, I was content to set up camp for the night alongside the bike path and jot a few notes in my journal before the sun went down. Strolling through the familiar streets of Troy and down memory lane, I decided to make a quick surprise visit to a friend's house to refresh my water bottles.

As with most of our friends in Troy, a casual knock on the garage door was the normal approach for familiar faces to announce their presence. Quickly, my friends Joe and Laurie came to the door and ushered me to the backyard where the intoxicating smell of barbecued chicken on the grill filled the air. They were entertaining guests this Sunday evening and insisted that I join them and their guests for dinner. They demanded that I scrap my plans for a water fill-up and instead put a glass of wine in my hands.

How could I refuse?

Hours later, a hot shower, a bellyful of food, and a bed brought this trip to a soft ending.

Some Final Thoughts

As most can imagine, the tedious work of converting one's inner thoughts to a published book while tending to life's other needs can drag out the progress of completion. To this end, I want to acknowledge those who helped me on my journey. I am grateful to each person who continually coached and prodded my progress.

First on any of my lists is my wife Laurie who helped me to maintain my voice throughout this work. In addition, her continued support through long days of my absenteeism and her willingness to singlehandedly take care of our family while I was out on the road has allowed me to creatively explore the country. Her sometimes critical and always loving view, not only of my eccentricities but also of my commitment to travel and writing, continues to stimulate conversation for us. These conversations resulted in a balanced perspective of what we believe the audience wants to read. At my day job, we call this WIFM, (what's in it for me). Hopefully, you found the WIFM value in reading this book.

Tom Hofbauer was my editor. His attention to detail and correctness provided a structure to my writing that allowed a conversational story to evolve. Similar to most athletic events, we regularly challenged each other with the goal of shaping this book to be the best that we could produce. Never more than a phone call away; Tom was quick to find solutions to my word blocks.

Susan Mangan helped coach and inspire a technical writer and engineer with a penchant for detail to shift from a writing style based on material found in the head to one based on sensual observations found in the heart. My transition to creative writing required a leap of faith that may have never happened without Susan's excitement for the written word. It is contagious and unparalleled.

Finally, Tom Moffitt, President of the Ohio to Erie Trail Board, has been a constant source of energy and access to the technical data of the OTET. I am appreciative to Tom and the numerous volunteers that have dedicated their time to establish and improve the OTET.

Care was taken to describe visual features and historic reference points along the OTET while enjoying bicycle travel. As the OTET continues to develop as a primary artery of bike travel across the state, there are plans afoot to connect other trails with US Bike Route 1. One such trail described in *A Path Through Ohio* is the Miami Valley Bikeway that connects out of Xenia. Each connection provides an opportunity to enhance the rider's experience by pushing into new areas of the state. While researching for historical context along the OTET, it was abundantly clear that there is a great deal more history to uncover as interest dictates. The Appendix provides a list of historical markers I found and photographed along the trail. Though not an all-inclusive list, it does provide a starting point with more to be added as other trail systems are connected.

Each week, I am pleasantly surprised to read in the local papers about interesting small businesses that got their start in Ohio or a piece of history that re-surfaces as a significant anniversary or an event that is a resemblance of today's events. Being aware of the local history on the route is one way to enrich the backdrop of any ride. The Ohio to Erie Bike Trail website is a useful resource which will provide you access to updated maps and resource detail as the trail evolves.

The events inspiring this travel journal occurred in 2014. Since then, numerous changes to the trail have occurred. However, as of this writing, the persons, the history, and the journey itself are frozen in time. Not to be defined by one trip alone, I have taken up my bike and pen again and have endeavored to ride around each of North America's Great Lakes. These travels will take me through some of this continent's most populated cities and around it's most pristine natural resource, accessible fresh water, which makes up 20% of the world's fresh water. This singular resource is increasingly in need of our protection to preserve it and it's an issue worth writing about.

Since the initial writing of *A Path Through Ohio,* I have participated in a group ride around Lake Ontario with friends. This well-thought-out ride required a yearlong strategy of gaining commitments, aligning schedules, and unifying equipment and resources. Through the development and execution of this strategy, I was inspired to create two important new Road Rules. Each new rule underscores the importance of planning your own "big hairy" adventure. Although both are related, each carries merit of its own.

Road Rule Number Fourteen, "Dream it - Plan it - Practice it - Do it", focuses on turning a dream or idea into a set of realistic and tangible actions that will help you make progress towards your dream adventure.

Road Rule Number Fifteen, "Define your trip goals in advance but be agile enough to change your goals", discusses how we measure success. When your adventure is over and the high fives and accolades are well behind you, how will you look back at all the achievements and distractions? Will you summarize the event as a success or will it be less than successful? Will you recommend to your friends that they try the same? What would you do differently?

I recently saw a bumper sticker on a car that summarized succinctly why bicycle travel has enticed me for so many years.

"Travel by four wheels transports the body. Travel by two wheels transports the soul."

I thought that this was a thoughtful way to conclude this adventure while allowing you to ponder the possibilities of your next adventure. As you do so, remember the following deeper benefits to adventure cycling.

It reverses the trend of consumerism and emphasizes conservation • *It* clears the forest of indecision and requires us to make decisions • *It* fills the valley of self-worth with hope and confidence • *It* makes straight the path of a singular goal.

Ride well and make your dreams a reality.

APPENDIX 1

Looney's Road Rules

Road Rule Number One: Start every day with a song.

"Begin the day with a friendly voice, a companion unobtrusive, plays that song that's so elusive, And the magic music makes your morning mood" (Rush, Permanent Waves).

I am a big fan of starting each day with the right attitude in order to gain peak performance from my body. Whether it is the ride into the office or shaking off last night's thundershower while holed up in a tent, the new day brings opportunities to meet new people or to explore one of earth's treasures. As any good athlete prepares for an event, the warm-up is the tool of choice to stretch the body and warm the muscles in preparation for the event. Similarly, the mind needs to warm up. Positive platitudes, visualization exercises, and music are the brain's favorite tools for programming. Although we're not all athletes, starting the day with a positive outlook allows the rider to hop on that saddle just one more time, shake off that cold morning chill, and start churning those pedals to the cadence of a familiar drum beat.

I once had the opportunity to watch the Team USA sprinters warm up for the day's practice at the US Olympic Training Center in Chula Vista, California. From a distance, I watched them jog through their drills on the 400-meter track. At the near end of the beautifully surfaced track was a five-story tower that supported a viewing box and a significant speaker system. As the sprinters concluded their warm-up drills, one came to the tower and blared two audio tracks. The first was a tape from an Olympic stadium with crowd noise as background and the other was the runner's favorite rap music. Inspired by this music, the team went to work immediately.

Road Rule Number Two. Make a journal entry daily.

"There are a thousand thoughts lying within a man that he does not know till he takes a pen to write." William Thackeray.

Summarize each day by making a conscious effort to capture the day's highlights or possibly the low points, the associated feelings, and the key learning. "Hell, I'll never do that again" may be just the note needed to prevent you from repeating the same mistake over. Each is a gem of an emotion to be recalled at a later point in time.

Journal writing in the privacy of your own space allows for free-flowing thoughts to be captured and, if desired, articulated more creatively at a later point. Surprisingly, some of my best moments of self-discovery and observation occur after a long day in the saddle with dinner in the tank and the evening sun fading on the horizon. Take the time to jot, draw, or scribble your likes and dislikes, how you felt, or maybe even a new bucket list idea. As Victor Frankl, a Holocaust survivor once wrote, "Writing allows us to free ourselves from our history". In part, I think he was trying to convey that the simple act of documenting our feelings allows us to move on in life to enjoy or suffer new feelings, making for a richer life experience.

———————————————

Road Rule Number Three: Sleep with one eye open.

"You must stop and turn to face the dragon, to realize he is made of paper" (Chinese Proverb)

In today's world of verbal diarrhea on TV and bad news which sells best, our society is swept into a condition of fear; fear of walking the dog around the block; fear to go to the "east side" or "that" place. Fortunately, the cyclist does not run into this amped shock culture very often. For some, their fears are more founded in urban America rather than the woods of rural America.

Yes, there are bears and deer and other wild critters out there that forage for food at night. In our mind's eye, we have a tendency to explode the snapping of a twig or a hearty snort of a buck as a threat and imminent danger that may be lurking in the dark. "Sleeping with one eye open" simply means to be aware of your surroundings and take appropriate precautions. Remove your food from your tent, don't camp near animal feces or tracks, and stay away from freshly dug holes or hollowed timber. Finally, when you first begin camping, you will likely only get partial sleep through most of your camp nights. These fears generally pass as your confidence grows with your capabilities and surroundings. The camping part of adventure cycling is not for everyone. Consequently, there are many reasonable options to pursue. Plan ahead. Make sure your accommodations are confirmed the day before you arrive. Get cleaned up and sleep well. You will have the same challenges the next day as those who chose the ground upon which to sleep.

I have the greatest regard for those who have responded to the call of adventure. Those of you who have experienced this form of travel will likely attest that there is a vast network of bike shops that exhibit a general openness to help a fellow traveler. You're never really alone. The sandbox in which you play is just a little larger than most others.

Road Rule Number Four: For every hill, there is an equal and opposite hill.

Having logged thousands of miles on bike and on foot, I have learned not to fight or become obsessed with the topography and the elements that Mother Nature and fate have put in my path. Standing in frustration at the base of a mountain or staring in the face of dark, foreboding clouds does not change the reality that you must either endure or go home. Rather, be prepared for the extremes and take action in advance to maintain reasonable comfort during tough times. For those of faith, these are the character-enriching experiences that you are in search of. It is God's way of shaping you to use your gifts, turning fear and humility into courage and accomplishment. The silver lining of each experience is that there is a downhill ride and a sunny side to each challenge.

Road Rule Number Five: Know thy food and water needs.

Dietary and hydration concerns are always prevalent when one is exposed to the elements regardless of whether that exposure is just for hours or for trips lasting multiple days. Of the two, hydration is your number one concern in order to maintain proper body fluid levels. I have noticed that the combination of exposure and exercise can best be compensated with up to one liter per hour of water. When urinating, look for a clear fluid as an indication of your success. I also alternate water with sports drinks when on a particularity long grind to help replace lost electrolytes.

The calories burned (CB) during a long day's journey is also an important statistic to watch while actively riding. There are many calculators on the Internet that estimate the amount of CB during exercise. I suggest consulting your doctor before embarking on a journey. There are many variables that dictate your physiological needs on a given day. There is much more science behind the maintenance of your physical needs. As you become familiar with any form of distance exercise, be aware of your unique needs and replace calories and fluids regularly. I prefer ice cream any time the opportunity avails itself.

Plan ahead, know the distances between stops and if they are greater than a couple of hours, plan to pack extra reserves. Through force of habit, I generally carry two water bottles and energy bars as a reserve. Let your body be your first indicator to replace fluids and fuel.

———————◦———————

Road Rule Number Six: Let go of the electronics, use your surroundings, and use your senses.

"Baby, be a simple, really simple man. Oh, be something you love and understand." Lynyrd Skynyrd, Simple Man

This is not about the resistance to using electronics or popular GPS and experience-enhancing tools. It is about raising your awareness to your experiences. As our technology gets better and better, it also insulates us from our immediate surroundings. It hides in plain sight and can make us oblivious to danger. If you're staring at your GPS, you're losing out not only on the immediate scenery but also may be unaware of that pothole in the road just 10 feet in front of you. Put the watch away. Watches are used for keeping appointments. Some of the best days on the road have a start and end point with the rising and setting of the sun. Allow the entire course of the day to be a series of random and unexpected events.

The last time I checked, your body will tell you when to eat, sleep, and relieve yourself. It's okay to find a park during a midday ride, pull up under a broad-leafed oak to take shelter from the mid afternoon sun, and just take a nap. You're on autopilot now. You may just find that the slice of freedom from your highly structured and complex "other life" is what you have been craving for years.

In case you were wondering, I am old school; maps and compass all the way.

Road Rule Number Seven: Riding alone doesn't mean you're lonesome.

Fellow cyclist Bob Howells once wrote, "When you travel as a group, you're viewed as a group. You're assumed to be collectively self-sufficient. When you're alone, others see you as a fellow human being. People readily share their humanity with you. The earth and the people within unfold in proportion to your openness to them. Each of us has travel preferences that may include solo riding, group riding, or even event riding. The solo option in cycling opens the door to new acquaintances that may change your way of thinking."

Road Rule number seven is not so much about riding alone as it is about knowing what you want from a ride and how to best achieve these desires. The seasoned traveler may be in search of a new destination such as an unexplored national park. The young adventurer may want to navigate across a trail with GPS and the athlete may want to pound out mega miles; like a hundred miles day. In the end, there is a personal reward for each type of cyclist whether in large groups or as a soloist. Determine your motivations for riding, pick the options that best suit your desired travel, and ride with purpose. The long miles in the saddle will teach you to appreciate your surroundings with all of your senses and challenge you to look into your soul.

Road Rule Number Eight: Know where you are and where you want to be. When in doubt, use multiple maps including state, local or trail.

The obvious reaction to this road rule is to employ the use of a GPS unit. However, many have experienced regions where even the best electronic devices lose reception or experience a blackout. Whether the GPS is your primary or secondary tool for navigation, it is important to know your bearings and to know that you're maintaining the planned trajectory or direction. Learn about the areas through which you will be traveling. Use natural features in your surroundings to keep your bearings correct.

While on a bicycle and generally in congested or urban environments, the need for confirming location checks increases when compared to the speed of a backpacker. There will be numerous challenges for the cyclists attempting to navigate through the congestion of information and traffic. Common mistakes on the cycling road include missed turns, hidden street signs, route numbers for road names, detours, and even good intentions but wrong directions. Each of these challenges can have a potentially disastrous effect.

Many years ago in rural Faulkton, South Dakota, I took a turn on an old county road, thinking that I could avoid a strong easterly head wind and later return to my east heading when the wind died down. Though the Triple AAA state maps showed my location and where I ultimately wanted to be, it certainly did not show the conditions I was about to experience along the way. What started as a formal asphalt road deteriorated progressively to the condition of a trail and I soon found myself in a fool's bet. Each reduction in road quality was met with the optimism that this was a temporary degradation and that the traveling surface would surely return to asphalt in the next mile. Twenty miles later, my wheels sinking in loose soil and surrounded by corn stalks, I was barely able to see the rooftop of the next farmhouse. Having made a decision to cut my losses, I found a farmer who admired my effort to visit him and he redirected me back down the road I had just traveled. I did return to town in time for lunch after a 40-mile mistake, much humbled and wiser rider.

So the point of this Road Rule is to use all of the available resources–maps, local people, and GPS. Keep yourself informed to the largest extent possible as to where you are and where you want to be.

————————•◦—————————

Road Rule Number Nine: Embrace your eccentricity.

Everyone has one.
Your mission is to find out what yours is.

It is truly an enlightening sensation to wake up every day in the outdoors with only one purpose–to find out what the day has in store for you. Some days are packed full of stimulation and others are... well... just plain boring. They could be flat, hot, and lacking companionship or they could be just a long, long grind. To the untrained mind, this can be pure torture and, quite honestly, the reason why endurance sport has a bad rap.

When in a rut, I have found a couple of practices to help break up the tedium of long distance riding. The first practice is something I label as associative thinking. Creating a hyper interest and curiosity in every facet of the ride leads to a more efficient performance but also breaks the monotony. Questions that come to mind include monitoring my

speed, ease of breathing, or the distance to the
core. In the meantime, the miles melt away.

nique used is known as dissociative thinking.

a little creative courage but is equally effective

redom. Your mind is a wonderful tool that can
launch a thousand thoughts and emotions from poetic verse
to favorite song lyric or a charming line from a movie. When
alone on the long, desolate road, you can conjure any rock
star you want to be. Go ahead and belt out a couple of
favorite tunes. So what if you're off key or miss a word or
two. It's the emotion from deep inside tied with the song that
brings a rush of feelings. Though I risk dating myself, you
may be surprised what comes from your soul, lying just
beneath your boredom–possibly a Bob Seger tune or a line
from Monty Python and the Holy Grail. For the intellectuals,
it could be reciting the Gettysburg Address. Unless you're a
karaoke regular, I recommend making sure there's plenty of
space between you and anyone in earshot.

**Road Rule Number Ten: Always leave a trail of where you've
been and where you're going.**

In the 2000s, a book titled *Between a Rock and a Hard Place*
written by adventurer Aron Ralston describes his survival
experience on a rock-climbing trip in Blue John Canyon in
Utah. In the course of his trip, his arm became pinched
between a sizeable rock formation and a large boulder.

Ralston found himself unable to extricate his arm from between the two surfaces. Even worse, he was stuck with limited supplies. The following six days became a gripping tale of survival. Aron later admitted that the whole ordeal could have been avoided if he had just let someone know where he was going and how long he planned to be out of town.

The point here is to keep in touch with someone while striking out on a new adventure. Self-reliance is important for all adventurers but an ounce of preparation such as a compiling a travel itinerary or carrying a charged cell phone can save your hide from the unexpected. By the way, I recommend the book, especially if you're an adrenaline junkie.

―――――――――――◦―――――――――――

Road Rule Number Eleven: Be an ambassador for cycling and be nice to strangers.

In other parts of the world where nomadic travel is a way of life, the traveler is an emissary carrying a message of peace or care for one family or another. In eastern Africa, an old Swahili proverb is commonly used to describe the role of the traveler; "Mgeni aje mwenyeji apone". This roughly translates to "When the guest visits, the host is healed". Many miles of travel have exposed me to those with a dream to be untethered from their life conditions, much as a touring cyclist is untethered from the office chair or work routine. As cyclists, we carry a rare trait of optimism no matter the condition. Yes, we can complain with the best of them but when it comes to enduring distress or physical hardship, the cyclist is equipped like no other. The optimism of the next sunny day, the next farmer's market (and the opportunity to gorge on food), or the next downhill cruise is always around the next corner and often are the stuff of which food dreams are made. With this positive outlook on life, the cycling tourist has a rare opportunity to influence others to experience their surroundings beyond the comfort of a car. The cycling tourist is an ambassador who awakens the possibility that a ride around the block, a ride to the next neighborhood, or a ride across town is achievable. Distant cycling at its core increases the confidence to be self-reliant and go the next mile.

Many years ago while riding through a small farming town in rural Wisconsin, I was coming to the end of a long day with my heavy load on two wheels. I was suddenly startled by a young boy who snuck up behind me on his Stingray bike. He was curious enough to ask, "Where ya going, mister?" As I explained my mission of riding through not just his state but many others as well, he blurted back that he wanted to do that some day. As the chitchat continued over the next couple of miles, we were as close as two kids dreaming about the future from the end of an old, wooden fishing pier. Shortly thereafter, he sped away. Some distance later, I found his bike on the side of the road. The boy and his family were nearby, out in front of their family farm and grocery. As I passed, they waved me down from their front porch and insisted that I select some fresh fruit and cheese from their grocery. This was a small but welcome bonanza for a calorie-craved cyclist. As I walked away from the barn, a faded sign advertising Colby Cheese caught my eye. As I packed up my bike with cheese, I could not help but wonder if this was part of the famed Colby Cheese family.

I don't know if the young rider ever took his Stingray cycling aspirations beyond the family farm but I do know he learned about dreaming big that day.

Road Rule Number Twelve: Stop the negative, replace with positive and realistically assess.

When working with the Boy Scouts as a troop leader, we often ended our long days by sitting around a campfire ring and sharing our thoughts about the day's strenuous hike or other events. This exercise was commonly known as "thorns, rose, and buds ". In turn, each scout would reflect on his likes, dislikes, and most importantly the opportunities that each hoped to see, do, or achieve in the coming days. Surprisingly, even on the most strenuous of days and in the most inclement conditions, each scout could dig deep enough to find one ember of hope that would keep him motivated to move forward.

When performing most physical activities, your mind is assessing your body and its performance. On a surface level, it may be a sore knee or a nagging hitch in a running stride. Each of the day's little events or environmental conditions are also continually being assessed and creating a disposition that can range from euphoric and positive to brooding and negative. Whatever the condition, it is important to be in tune with these changes in mood and outlook.

To stay realistically positive is to recognize the negative elements causing your poor outlook and objectively identify a positive outcome with your available skills and resources. Even when your immediate future looks gloomy, assess all of your skills, your resources, and your equipment when trying to determine a course of action that will lead you to a better outcome. Stay calm and generally unemotional. Think through your options, determine your corrections, and don't procrastinate in taking action.

Road Rule Number Thirteen: Meet someone interesting daily.

**Allow conversations to develop.
These are the gems of the day.**

When I first biked across the country as a young man, the bike and the travel became a vehicle for seeing national parks and recognizable sights. Looking back after 30-years of travel by bike, I realized that I missed a sizeable portion of self-discovery and purpose for the ride. Replaying the mental tape many years later, the memories that come back in full color are the people that I met and the impressions that they left on me. Don't get me wrong; the photographs and postcard images are all equally beautiful and serene but the brief acquaintances with other human beings carries an emotional context that remains etched in our memory for years afterward.

With many miles of cycle travel behind me, I have experienced highs and lows from each and what I have concluded to be the most memorable achievements are not the places I've been nor the miles I've ridden nor the pain I have endured. The memories most cherished are those that involve human contact and the brief exchange of ideas with people from different backgrounds.

———————○———————

Road Rule Number Fourteen:
Dream it – Plan it – Practice it – Do it

Adventure comes in many shapes and sizes and each adventure offers the aspiration to press the limits of physical comfort and mental toughness. Most adventures start as a kernel of an idea influenced by an article in the paper, events that we've encountered in our daily lives, or a challenge laid down by a friend. The kernels are endless. What turns a dream into reality is hard-core planning. This kind of planning accounts for every detail, bringing you closer to a crystalized picture of the target. Planning requires you to take that bold step of converting a "cool idea" into a written statement. As that written statement hangs on your mirror or some other conspicuous location, your mind subconsciously gnaws away at the details. Gradually over time, your plan starts to develop in detail and color. Keep adding detail to your plan until the point where you feel a personal commitment to the plan and can willingly describe it to a friend or confidant. With an internalized commitment and some constructive feedback, you're ready to go to the next phase. Practice it.

While the planning phase allows you to visualize your "Big Hairy Plan" (BHP), the "practice it" phase now consumes your conscious thoughts. You take actions to study route maps, create gear lists, and most importantly, go out and ride for the exercise and mental preparation. All of these actions are building upon your BHP and helping you internalize the vision that you have. During the "practice it" phase, continue to talk to your friends; "Here's what I am thinking, what do you think?" Each conversation continues to build your commitment to the BHP and at the same time sends a signal to the rest of your inner circle of friends, "I'm gonna do this". After months of planning and preparation, you're now on day one of your BHP. This is the "do it" phase. At this time, you should feel confident that you've put in the hard work of planning and practice. You may feel a little nervous about some detail you missed but by and large, your BHP is solid. As the miles roll along on day one, you will feel an abundance of excitement as the strings of responsibility slip away. And your confidence will continue to grow mile after mile.

Road Rule Number Fifteen: Define your trip goals in advance but be agile enough to change your goals.

The cornerstone of every adventurer is to balance the elation of achievement with the risk of not being successful. Underestimate the risk or overestimate your ability and problems will start to appear. Fortunately, we each have the ability to define the boundaries or goals of our adventure. We also have the ability to change the goal. After all, it is "your goal".

In a prior life as a running/marathon coach, I prescribed a structured, three-layer goal-setting expectation for each student. In other words; "following a race, what three outcomes from the race would make you feel like you accomplished your mission?" Too many times, we don't carefully think through why we are investing enormous training hours and sacrifices and to what end. The "why am I doing this marathon" gets lost in the busyness of training. I once had a runner who had just completed an admirable marathon and immediately asked, "How did I do, coach?" Trying to get the runner to identify with the deeper meaning of the question, I responded, "How did you think you did?" Though a simplistic example, this runner had not defined a successful outcome and after a couple more questions, this runner felt a little more satisfied with her race. The runner has the opportunity to set goals on many different levels of race performance. As an example, three different outcomes for a goal might be to a) just finish the race or b) finish with a select time in mind or c) finish in the top 10% in an age group. This skill can easily become a valuable tool in defining success for any adventure.

Similar to the runner, the adventure cyclist should establish expectations in a way that defines a successful outcome. In business terms, we call these SMART objectives; Specific, Measurable, Actionable, Realistic, and Time-bounded. A quick Google search on SMART goals will provide a wealth of information on how to establish and manage your trip goals.

A final note on goal setting

As important as it is to define the goals of your adventure, do not lose sight of the fact that these are self-made and left up for interpretation as the adventure unfolds. There are an unlimited number of events that may cause you to change your goal. Be flexible with your goals to the point that your decisions to change are simply alterations to enhance your safety or experience from the original design. For me, I generally abandon my "daily miles" goal when I meet someone new or interesting. Establish your goals but be flexible enough to modify them as the conditions around you warrant.

APPENDIX 2

Cycle Touring Essentials (for three-season travel)

The Ten Essentials:

1. Directions: Maps (state, local, trail views), compass, GPS.
2. Water: Two bottles minimum and a way to purify (if needed). Refill at every opportunity.
3. Reserve food: High-energy bar, jerky, trail mix, dried fruit and nuts.
4. Clothing: Wicking layer, thermal layer, shell layer.
5. First Aid:(basic) Ointment, aspirin, petroleum jelly, diaper rash cream, sanitizer, band-aids.
6. Mechanical: Multi purpose tool, tire irons, chain tool, knife, spare inner tube.
7. Lighting: Front and rear lighting, spare headlamp as a backup.
8. Shelter: Vented three-season tent.
9. Sleep gear: Sleeping bag and pad.
10. Prevention: Sunscreen, bug repellant, body cream.

The Other Essentials:

- Eye protection: Sunglasses.
- Helmet: Properly fitted.
- Eating utensils: Plate, cup, spork (combination spoon and fork), bowl, scrubber.
- Toiletries: Toilet paper, soap, toothpaste, toothbrush, washcloth, towel, hand sanitizer. Include other items as required by the traveler.
- Cooking equipment: Lighter, wet-proof matches, stove, fuel, small cook pot set.
- General adventure equipment: Small roll of utility tape, permanent marker, 25-foot parachute chord, 8-inch zip ties, whistle, mirror, and plastic garbage bag.

Community Gear:

- Stove and fuel: fire-starting items.
- Cooking gear: Pots, large spoon, knife, can opener, cutting board/mat.
- Food supply as per travel plan.
- Tarp/poles (if you anticipate inclement weather).

Things to Prepare:

- Mechanically sound bike including spokes, chain, brakes, trued wheels, tires, and lubrication.
- Properly loaded panniers that are balanced front and back and side-to-side. Two panniers in back. (Two panniers in the front of the bike are optional based on travel duration). Pack for three changes of clothes if traveling for longer than a week.
- Gear weight: Estimate 35-50 lbs. depending on size or person, duration of trip, and accessory selection.
- Electronics: Portable battery charger (for when power is inaccessible), charge cord, waterproof bag.
- Essentials to be keep accessible: First aid, rain gear, fire starter.
- Keep dry: Sleeping bag, clothing layers, hat and gloves.
- Ride gear: Two changes each: shorts, shirt, socks (alternate and wash), walk-able bike shoes.
- Travel gear: (street clothes) one each of pants, shirt, sneakers, socks.

Things to Know/Remember:

- Physical limitations: Overall fitness and limitations, dietary, medical, allergies. Plan on taking walk breaks every 20 miles or after an hour of saddle time.
- First-aid skills: Priority of administering first aid including ABC: Airway, Bleeding, Circulatory.

- Orienteering skills: Maps/compass, GPS. (Know where you are and where you're going).
- Local dangers: Poisonous/dangerous animals, plant life, traffic, road shoulder condition.
- Geographical challenges: Mountains, water resources, ferries, bridges, and country borders/passport requirements.
- Weather conditions: Take shelter as necessary. Hypothermia in the summer is a real concern during inclement conditions.
- Civilization checkpoints: Anticipate cities, highways, avoid congestion and high-use roads.
- Three layer clothing system: Wicking, thermal, vented shell.
- Base food: On longer rides each rider should keep a spare soup/oatmeal package for at least two meals for emergency issues. Keep mixed nuts, dried fruit in reserve. There are numerous options for sport bars, and gel's if desired.
- Financial considerations: Credit card, cash, exchange rates, and back-up plan.

Things To Do:

- Notification: Designate a contact person who will know where you are going and your expected return time.
- Prepare a travel plan: With group or contact person, establish checkpoints, exchange phone numbers, and notify authorities as required.
- If you become lost: S.T.O.P. - Stop, Think, Observe, Plan.
- Observe basic personal cleanliness routines. Cleanliness promotes good hygiene and positive attitude for the next day's ride. (Wet towel wipes to a warm shower).
- Be visible on the road: Lights, reflectors, vest, flags, and clothing.

- Use proper hand signal and audio pronouncements: "car back, on your left, passing, stopping, slowing, clear left/clear right".

Low Impact (ethical) Camping:

- Get permission on private or restricted property.
- Do not litter and pick up litter from others.
- Stay on trail, don't cut the switchbacks.
- Give right-of-way to uphill, motorized vehicles, and wild animals.
- Camp at least 200 feet from established waterway, other campsites.
- Avoid high ridges, riverbeds or other dangerous locations.
- Avoid digging trenches or rearranging fragile terrain.
- Remove food from tents. String food up at night.

APPENDIX 3

Mark's Current Memberships:

- **Ohio to Erie Trail:** www.ohiotoerietrail.org
- **Rails to Trails Conservancy:** www.railstotrails.org
- **Adventure Cycling Association:** www.adventurecycling.com
- **Warm Showers:** www.warmshowers.org
- **AAA Auto Club:** www.aaa.com

Other Regional Bicycle path information:

- **Ohio Erie Canal Way:** www.ohioanderiecanalway.com
- **Bed and Breakfast Biking:** bbbiking.com

- **Great Ohio Bicycle Adventure, GOBA:**
  www.goba.com

List of Ohio Historical Markers Along this Ride:
1. 110-18 West Side Market (Cleveland)
2. 80-18 South Park Village and Whittlesey Tradition (Independence)
3. 1-76 Ohio Erie Canal, Lock Number 4 of 142 (Canal Fulton)
4. 47-25 Big Darby, Little Darby Creeks
5. 2-42 Little Indian Fields, Johnny Appleseed (Knox County)
6. 9-21, Stage Coach Station (Sunbury)
7. 3-38 Holmes County Draft Riot
8. 10-29 Galloway House
9. 21-29 First Courthouse of Green County
10. 57-9 Site of first NFL game (Dayton)
11. 10-97 Village of Tadmor (Tipp City)
12. 24-25 Miami & Erie Canal Lock 15 (Tipp City)

Reference:

For Ohio to Erie Trail Maps go to: www.ohiotoerietrail.org

- Map One: Cleveland, Akron, Massillon, Fredericksburg, and Killbuck
- Map Two: Danville, Mt. Vernon, and Sunbury
- Map Three: Columbus, London, and Xenia
- Map Four: Loveland to Cincinnati

Ohio to Erie Trail & Miami Valley Bikeway map courtesy of Robert Niedenthal.

Miami Valley Bikeways go to: www.miamivalleytrails.org Provides information about each of the RailTrails and other multi-use trails centered on Dayton and Xenia.

Glaser, Susan (2014, April 22). New Map helps bikers navigate the Ohio to Erie Trail; plus GOBA deadline approaches. Cleveland Plain Dealer. Retrieved from http://www.cleveland.com/travel/index.ssf/2014/04/new _map_helps_bikers_navigate.html

Allen W. Eckert's *The Frontiersmen*. Ashland: Jessie Steward Foundation, 2001. Print

Peter Jenkins, *A Walk Across America*. New York: Harper Collins Publishers, Inc., 1979. Print

Rush. *Spirit of Radio*. Mercury Records 1980, Album.

Bob Seger. *Traveling Man*. Capitol 1975, Album

Foreigner. *I Want To Know What Love Is*. Atlantic 1984

John Denver. *Take Me Home, Country Roads*. RCA 1971

Glen Campbell. *Rhinestone Cowboy*. Capitol 1975

Kenny Rogers. *The Gambler*. United Artists 1978

Daryl Hall and John Oates. *Lost that Loving Feeling*. RCA Records 1980

REO Speedwagon. *Keep Pushin*. Epic Recording 1977.

Bob Howell, *Touring Solo*, Bicycle Rider January/February 1986. Print